W9-AUO-035

MR. CSI

MR. CSI

HOW A VEGAS DREAMER MADE A KILLING
IN HOLLYWOOD, ONE BODY AT A TIME

ANTHONY E. ZUIKER

HARPER

An Imprint of HarperCollins*Publishers*
www.harpercollins.com

HarperCollins books may be purchased for educational, business, or
sales promotional use. For information, please write:
Special Markets Department, HarperCollins Publishers,
10 East 53rd Street, New York, NY 10022.

FIRST EDITION

Designed by Willaim Ruoto

Library of Congress Cataloging-in-Publication Data

Zuiker, Anthony E.
Mr. CSI : how a Vegas dreamer made a killing in Hollywood, one body at a time
/ Anthony E. Zuiker.
p. cm.
Summary: "A wrenching memoir in which the creator of *CSI: Crime
Scene Investigation*, one of the most popular shows of all time, applies
forensic techniques to his estranged father's suicide and his own
unlikely rise in Hollywood"—Provided by publisher.
ISBN 978-0-06-172549-4 (hardcover)
1. Zuiker, Anthony E. 2. Authors, American—20th century—
Biography. 3. Fathers and sons—United States—Biography.
4. Television producers and directors—United States—Biography.
5. CSI, crime scene investigation (Television program) I. Title.
PS3626.U35A3 2011
791.45'72—dc23 2011018791

11 12 13 14 15   OV/RRD   10 9 8 7 6 5 4 3 2 1

For Eddie

1974

CONTENTS

MR. CSI

PART I

THE POLICE
REPORT

LAS VEGAS POLICE DEPARTMENT

Crime Scene Investigation Summary
Date: January 10, 2005
Address: [REDACTED]

DETAILS

At the request of apartment complex
manager, officers were summoned late
morning to assist in entering unit 6A
after the occupant failed to respond
to manager's repeated attempts to make
contact.

ADDITIONAL DESCRIPTION

Officers arrived in front of the two-
story apartment complex at 9:50 AM.
The residential street was quiet, with
no traffic. The complex manager and his
wife, both in their 60s, exited from
their front unit and flagged the officers.
They guided the officers to ground
floor unit 6A, explaining they were
worried about the victim. They had not
seen him for several days. They tried
calling, but without a response. They
also knocked on his door, again with no
response. Fearful, they called Las Vegas
Police Department.

Arriving officers broke through front
door with minimal damage and intrusion

into the scene, and were able to visually encounter the victim slumped on the sofa, clearly dead. Officers turned on lights and saw the victim was male.

Manager identified the victim as the occupant, after which the manager and his wife returned to their apartment, where they explained the victim had been a tenant for three years and worked as a handyman. He had done odd jobs for them in the past, they said. Neither recalled the last time they had seen him, though they remembered noticing a flickering TV light in the window the night before.

Officers noted the television was turned on when they entered apartment. They found the victim had suffered severe head wounds. Victim, wearing white underwear, was found lying on his back, his torso twisted, with his head over the side facing north and his feet facing southeast. He was holding a shotgun in his right hand, with the barrel pointed toward his head. There was a large stain of dried blood and fragments of skull scattered in a semi-circular area to the left of the body.

Officers secured the scene and notified homicide division and LV County coroner.

PENDING TASK

Notify next of kin.

PART II

THE FACTS OF LIFE (AND DEATH)

JANUARY 9, 2005

The night before my father killed himself I attended the People's Choice Awards. It wasn't my first awards show. Nor was it my last. But I can't imagine another one ever being as significant, though it was more for the marker in my life it became rather than for the hardware I picked up.

The event was held in Pasadena, at the Civic Auditorium, which, barring traffic, was about forty-five minutes from my twenty-fourth-floor suite at the Universal Sheraton, where I lived while my shows, *CSI, CSI: Miami,* and *CSI: NY,* were in production.

On weekends and during the off-months, I lived with my wife and two sons in Las Vegas.

According to the People's Choice Awards invitation, the doors closed at 5 p.m. As I pulled out of the Sheraton, I checked my watch. It was one.

I didn't need a four-hour cushion. I left early so I could stop at a bar near the auditorium and spend a couple of hours watching a football game. With three TV series in production, those few hours of downtime with a beer and the NFL were my vacation, my trip to the French Riviera.

I got to the bar in half an hour. Inside, my eyes quickly adjusted to the relative darkness and I claimed a stool with a good view of the screen. With days that were scheduled, then overscheduled, and then changed depending on what happened on the sets, and nights that were also jammed with research and rewrites, I savored the first sip of a cold beer and the sight of football on a big screen.

Soon I started up a conversation with the bartender, a thick, sandy-haired guy who looked like he was between college and a career. I remembered the feeling. We talked about the game, which I had a bit of money on, but after he found out my connection to the three shows, he grilled me about crimes, murder, corpses, maggots, cops, and his two favorite TV characters—Gil Grissom and Catherine Willows.

Even though I was on a self-declared two-hour leave of absence, I was happy to oblige. I've always appreciated the connection people have with these shows and the characters. Those of us involved in the *CSI* franchise could go almost anywhere in the world and find fans with opinions and questions. Once, one of our producers was grilled on a beach in Spain about blood-splatter theory. Here in the bar it was no different. As we talked, I noticed most of the half-dozen guys near us were trying to eavesdrop.

"So you just thought of those shows?" the bartender asked. "Just one day you said, 'I've got an idea for a TV series about CSIs.' And that was it?"

"It's a great cast and I have some exceptional partners," I said.

"But it came out of your head?" he persisted.

I shrugged.

"Holy shit."

"I know," I said.

"You're rolling in it, right?"

"I'm lucky."

"Dude, let me buy you a drink," he said.

"No thanks," I said. "I have a long night ahead of me."

I explained about the People's Choice Awards.

"I don't know what you're up against, but *CSI* ought to win," he said.

"They tell a few people ahead of time to make sure they show up," I said.

"So *CSI* wins?" he asked.

I nodded.

"Congratulations," he said.

"Thanks."

He wiped down the counter with a white towel, provided refills to a couple of the other guys, and checked on the bottles lined up behind the bar. I could see he took pouring booze seriously. He was also good at making small talk, the kind of skill that makes a bar a welcome refuge from the outside world. Two brothers owned the place, he told someone. I glanced around the joint, then looked back up at the TV and got involved in the game again. During a commercial, the bartender stepped back in front of me.

"So those shows must be pretty fun?" he asked.

"Yeah," I said.

Unable to help himself, he asked about *CSI* stars William Petersen and Marg Helgenberger, as well as David Caruso from *Miami* and Gary Sinise from *New York*, plus a few others. He was a diehard. He forced me to remember storylines from previous seasons, little details, and questions that I tend to forget after the shows are written and produced. Each episode is a new challenge, and after we wrap I step back and breathe, and in that breath much of the struggle evaporates, or gets parked in a box in the back of my brain, before it's on to the next one.

But hey, if this guy wanted to talk about episode 19 of season two, "Stalker"—a show in which a woman is found dead in her apartment and the position reminds Nick Stokes of nightmares he's had—I was willing to call up memories of writing it with Danny Cannon, and explain to this guy that the idea was a combination of imagination and newspaper headlines. What if your nightmares were true? What if they happened and you found out about them after the fact—after the deadly fact?

"You mind me asking questions?" the bartender asked.

"No, not at all," I said.

I enjoy talking about writing almost as much as I like to write. Both take you to places you could only imagine, or didn't want to imagine. If I have a passion, it's work, immersing myself in the creative process. It's something I have to do because I can't *not* do it. Getting paid to do something I love is the biggest luxury in my life. I'm constantly aware of it, and appreciative, because I know the stakes. Like most everyone, I work to put a roof over my family's heads and food on the table, and some security in the bank. But for me, writing is also about figuring out issues beyond the work. My work isn't just about creating stories for a TV series. It's about creating my life, a life that is radically different from the one I knew before *CSI*. It's not a job or a lifestyle. It's an obsession.

I probably got carried away talking to the bartender about work. But then a new voice entered the conversation. I turned to my left. The guy from two stools over had moved closer. He was thin but muscular, midfifties, with white hair and a mustache. He tapped a quarter on the counter to get my attention.

"Sorry for butting in, but I heard you talking and can't resist," he said. "I want to know how the hell you think of a show like *CSI*."

"It's a long story," I said. "I mean, you don't just *think* of it. You get an idea and then put it together."

He ordered a beer and scooped up a handful of nuts from a new bowl.

"I'm a retired cop," he said. "I never miss any of the shows. I give you credit for getting it right."

"Thanks," I said.

"Anyone in your family cops?" he asked.

I shook my head no.

He considered my answer.

"Well, your old man's still got to be proud of you."

2

I nodded my head to the side and changed the conversation. Football was less complicated. My relationship with my dad, if it even qualified as a relationship, wasn't anything I wanted to get into here at the bar.

In talking about what motivated me to work hard, I spilled a few bits about my old man. That was plenty. I wanted to stay in a casual, pre-party mood if possible.

Ironically, up on the TV, the announcers talked about Colts quarterback Peyton Manning and his close relationship with his father, Archie, a former NFL great himself. I knew almost as much about Archie Manning as I did about my father, maybe more.

The former cop next to me turned out to have ridden motorcycles. In his off-hours he worked on TV and movie sets, a lucrative activity for off-duty LAPD officers. He had stories of his own, stories that went beyond Hollywood. His old man, he said, had also been a cop—and a drinker. He told part of that story, which took a few sad turns.

While listening, I reached into my pocket, found a pair of dice that I had stuck in there, and set them on the bar in front of me. Out of habit, I turned them over, creating different combinations. I've done this since childhood, when I got hooked on the odds of different numbers coming up, when I used to wonder, what were the chances?

For me, the dice were always more about the possibilities than anything else. But they also reminded me of my past. I could be anywhere in the world and as soon as I pulled them out I'd be transported back to the smoky, crowded casinos of my youth, back before that, even—back to my childhood, when I wondered, what were the chances of doing it better, of making it? Perhaps in a subconscious way they were reminders that I was never going to make a clean break from my past no matter how many shows I got on the air. Or maybe it was the other way around—a reminder of how far away I'd gotten.

I preferred to think about those dice simply as they were, implements that created the excitement of possibilities. Like watching a football game on TV. You had two teams and countless variables that affected the odds of one team winning over another. On any given day anything was possible. The same was true in business and life. Everything is a roll of the dice.

"What are the odds?" chimed the bartender, entering the conversation late.

"For what?" I asked.

"Anything," he said with a shrug.

"Well, you can figure out the odds of most things," I said. "Take these dice." I gave them a roll. "With one, you have six different possibilities. With two, you have thirty-six."

He scratched his head.

"I was never good at math," he said.

I went over it again, explaining that the probability of a combination of two dice adding up to seven was highest, that six and eight were the next likeliest, and so on down to the long shots, two, three, and twelve.

"I bet you do pretty well at the craps table," he said.

"I'm not much of a gambler," I said.

"I get it," he said, smiling. "You know the odds."

"Yeah, I guess," I said. "But really, too much of life is already a roll of the dice."

3

"Talk about a roll of the dice," the ex-cop said. "Look at that."

He thrust his arm onto the bar top and pushed up his sleeve, revealing a large, thick, pink scar. It looked like a subcutaneous caterpillar, about six inches long.

"A couple more millimeters, the bullet hits my artery and I bleed to death before they get me to the hospital. What are the odds I'm that lucky?"

"Did you have your armor on?" I asked.

"Yes, sir," he said.

"Were you in a defensive position?"

"By the book."

"Okay, so you're putting the odds in your favor the best you can," I said.

"I see what you're saying."

"The only time in our lives when the odds are incalculable, at least in terms of anything we can influence, is when we're born. That is the ultimate roll of the dice. After that we have the option, if not the opportunity, to at least try to put the odds in our favor."

"What about luck?" he asked.

I laughed.

"Luck is always part of the equation."

4

The People's Choice Awards was much less of a philo-sophical adventure than the bar, though it turned out to be a night of mixed results.

Outside the auditorium, I walked the red carpet with Billy and Marg, answering questions from the press and posing for photos. Later, I joined them and the rest of the *CSI* crew onstage to accept the award as TV's favorite drama.

Unfortunately, *CSI: NY* lost out to *Desperate House-wives* as TV's favorite new drama.

My wife, Jennifer, was mad when I talked to her later that night. I pretended to be upset, too. Then we laughed.

Award shows were fun, but with two hit series on prime-time television I had already won the most impor-tant prize—the opportunity to do the work that I loved.

5

JANUARY 10, 2005

It was midmorning, and I was in my office, the back room of a two-story bungalow on CBS's Radford lot in Studio City. The studio was home to about twenty TV shows. You couldn't step outside without seeing a crew set up to shoot. My office was relatively small, with a large desk, a couple of chairs, and a sofa. The walls were decorated with posters from all three *CSI* shows, and I had several vintage pinball machines in the corner that I liked to play.

But, *play*?

What was that? Who had the time?

On this particular morning, like every other morning, I was reading a script from an upcoming episode of *CSI: NY* and making notes on a yellow legal pad. I was intensely focused on the page and visualizing the action. I barely noticed when my assistant, Orlin, slid a pink message slip onto the corner of my desk.

"Espresso?" he asked.

"No thanks," I said.

A few minutes later, Orlin returned with an espresso anyway. After taking a sip, I glanced at the message slip, expecting it to be a CBS executive checking on the progress of one of the episodes or offering notes on the latest script we'd already submitted.

I was wrong. The message was from Daniel Holstein, a senior crime scene investigator with the Las Vegas Metropolitan Police Department. Daniel was also the real-life inspiration for *CSI*'s Gil Grissom.

He called once or twice a year, either to ask about the spread in a USC game or find out when I would be in Vegas so we could have lunch, catch up, and smoke cigars. This time was different.

When I called him back, I could tell from the tone of his voice that he wasn't just checking in.

"Listen, do you have some time to talk?" he asked.

"Yeah," I said.

He was quiet for a minute. I heard papers shifting on his desk.

"Do you know an Eddie Zuiker?" he asked.

Eddie Zuiker.

"Yeah, I know him," I said.

Eddie Zuiker was my father.

I couldn't remember the last time I'd spoken to him, and now, with Daniel on the phone, I had the sense I'd never speak to him again.

"Why do you want to know?" I asked. "Is he dead?"

I already knew the answer. Why else was a Vegas CSI calling about him?

"Yes," Daniel said. "He's dead."

"What's the story?" I asked. "What happened?"

"Hold on—I'm going to let you talk to another CSI about what they found."

I don't know why, but I didn't expect a woman's voice. After a moment, though, it didn't matter. The facts were the facts.

"Mr. Zuiker, this is Officer Theresa Zito from the crime lab. I hate to be delivering bad news about—"

"Daniel told me."

"Your father," she said. "He was found dead this morning in his apartment complex." She paused, then added, "It looks like it was a suicide."

"Okay." I took a deep breath. "How?"

"A gun," she said.

"Where?" I asked. "I mean, where'd he do it?"

"At his apartment," she said.

I had no idea where he lived. Except for a phone message here or there and a couple times when our paths had inadvertently crossed, we had barely spoken since I was sixteen.

"Where was that?"

"Over on Las Vegas Boulevard," she said. "Next to the Harbor Apartments."

Officer Zito spoke in the kind of slow, measured, and clinical tone that had captivated me when I first researched *CSI*. Although typically describing the most horrendous circumstances, such officers were always direct. There was no hedging or hiding. Without emotion, they focused on the facts. The facts always told the best story.

"Look, just give it to me," I said. "What happened?"

"The method was inner oral," she said.

I understood the code. My dad had put a gun in his mouth and pulled the trigger.

I gave Officer Zito my phone number and said I'd return to Las Vegas right away. My head was spinning as I hung up. I looked at the papers on my desk, then stared down at the floor and breathed slowly. When I looked up again, Orlin was walking into my office with *CSI: NY* executive producer Pam Veasey. With one look at me, they knew something was wrong, and they froze.

"Are you okay?" Pam asked.

"I was just informed that my dad killed himself."

"What?" she said.

"Oh my God," Orlin said. "Is that why Daniel—"

I nodded.

"I'm sorry," Pam said.

"We were estranged," I told them. "He lived in Vegas."

"How?" she asked.

"With a sawed-off shotgun," I said. "Inner oral. He put the thing in his mouth and pulled the trigger."

"Jesus."

The three of us were silent.

What is one supposed to say?

I asked Orlin to book me on the next couple of flights to Vegas. I wasn't sure which one I could make. Pam sat down across from me. I continued to stare at the edge of my desk without seeing anything beyond the jumble of thoughts reeling through my head. I hadn't seen my father for more than twenty-five years, but my instinct was to get there, to Vegas, and do something.

I began formulating a list. I had to get on a plane, call my wife, call my mother, and then . . . well, I didn't know what.

I knew there were things you were supposed to do when a parent died. Ordinarily those were things you learned and planned during and after an illness. What about a parent who took his own life? What about a parent you hadn't actually seen in years?

I shook my head at the irony. I'd spent five years writing about dead bodies, but I had no idea what I was supposed to do with my father's. I knew the routines the CSIs followed. I knew my dad's body would have been taken from his apartment to the coroner's office, where it would stay until the next of kin claimed it. I was the next of kin. It was my turn, and I didn't know what to do.

Dealing with Eddie's dead body didn't bother me as much as the thought of dealing with his life. He had killed himself. The deal was done. But now I had to wade into his life, clean up his affairs, and confront this man whom I had avoided for my entire adult life.

Who knew what I was going to learn about him? Who knew what I was going to have to face about myself?

My office was silent. Pam stared at me, waiting for a response. I was having a hard time focusing on anything.

Too many thoughts were vying for attention in my head. As one of the show's executive producers, I was supposed to be in control and know the answers. But I couldn't even pretend to have a grip on anything. If I had tried to fake it, Pam would've called me on it, as friends are supposed to do.

"I'm sorry," I said.

I was going to have to leave work for a few days. I felt guilty about dumping my share of the work on her.

"Don't apologize to me," she said. "Can I do anything? Can I help?"

A twenty-year veteran of the business, Pam had come to *CSI: NY* early in its first season when I was struggling as the show runner. She'd helped put it on solid ground. I appreciated her then and now even more than she knew. A TV show is at its core an exercise in collaboration. Like life.

"I want you to know that I think you're a great talent," I said. "In case I never thanked you for everything you've done, thank you. Thank you for making this show great."

"Anthony," she said. "Your dad—"

"I just wanted you to know," I interrupted. "I really respect what you do, what you're able to do."

"Go do what *you* have to do," she said. "Don't worry about work. Go deal with your life."

8

From then on, I was a man in motion. I grabbed my bag, got in the car, and headed to Burbank airport. I called my wife from the car. She was shocked as I filled her in on the few details I knew.

Less than ninety minutes later, I was on a plane to Vegas, staring out the window at large white clouds billowing across the sky like an armada of tall ships. Our descent was through hot thermals that made the ride feel like we were bouncing down a flight of stairs until we were on the ground.

I called my mom, who lived in town, and told her to put her husband, David, on the phone as well.

"Why?" she asked. "What's wrong?"

"Just get him," I said.

When they were both on the phone I told them the news. My mom gasped.

"David, make sure she's okay."

"I'm fine," she said. "What happened?"

"He killed himself."

"Oh my God."

I told her that I was already in Vegas and on my way to his apartment. She asked me to pick her up. Like me, she had lost track of where my father lived and rarely spoke to him anymore, but she wanted to be there, too. I said I'd pick her up.

They'd divorced when I was five years old, but Eddie still cast a large shadow over her life, as he did mine.

After I picked her up, we drove across town in silence until I pulled up in front of his apartment. It was a plain, two-story, L-shaped stucco building. Everything from the structure to the grass out front was parched and weathered from the desert sun.

My mom stood in front of the car, shaking her head.

"This man once lived in a beautiful home," she said.

"I thought it was a mansion," I said. "He used to boast about heating his pool year-round."

"I had no idea he lived like this," she said.

Before we went inside, I reached into my pocket and took out two pair of latex gloves and crime scene booties I had brought from *CSI*'s prop department. I offered a pair to my mom. Although my dad's body had been removed, I had no idea what we might find inside. For all I knew, there was going to be gazpacho all over the walls.

I warned my mom and opened the door. I took a few tentative steps into the room before holding up my hand. "Let's just take a moment," I said.

Late afternoon light filtered in through the drape-covered windows and the open door behind us. I felt like I was Grissom in the *CSI* episode "Crate 'n Burial" when he tells a rookie cop not to turn on the lights because he wanted to see how the criminal had left it.

"I want to see how Eddie left it," I said.

Or did I?

Too late for that.

My eyes went straight to the couch where he shot himself. To the left was a splatter of blood that cascaded up the wall—the gazpacho. Over to the right, near his piece-of-crap TV, I noticed several chunks of head, brain, and scalp. I thought I might get sick. I took a deep breath and turned on the light. That helped.

I heard Grissom's voice in my head: "Concentrate on what cannot lie. The evidence."

He'd collected about two hundred empty Bic disposable lighters in a large bowl that sat on top of the coffee table in front of the couch where he'd spent his last moments. In each one of them the flame was gone. I didn't need Grissom to point out the symbolism. He had an old PC on a table, and nearby were boxes filled with papers, bills, and correspondence. Those were his records, the facts of his life—at least some of them—as Grissom might've said. I also saw dozens of magazines in the corner. Were they saved? Or were they discards that never made it out the front door?

My attention turned elsewhere when the blinking red light across the room caught my eye. It was his phone answering machine. The old-fashioned kind, circa sometime in the '80s; the kind with a cassette tape. It was on the tile counter between the living room and the kitchen. I removed the tape, put it in my pocket, and continued into the kitchen. I checked inside the fridge. The shelves were bare. No food, nothing to eat, no plans to stick around for another meal. He'd left a large frying pan on top of the stove with about an inch of bacon grease in it and a sink full of dirty dishes.

I wondered when he'd given up. It appeared to have been a while ago.

Eddie was living here?

"What?" my mom asked, as if hearing my thoughts.

"Nothing," I said. "It's just . . . this is pretty bad."

I turned around and noticed all the nautical tchotchkes he had scattered around, little captain's heads, boats, and sharks' teeth—all things I remembered from his mansion days.

"Mom, do you remember this stuff?" I asked. "Do you remember how much Eddie loved the sea?"

"Yes," she said through her hand, which was covering her mouth.

His bedroom, in contrast to the disarray of the living room and kitchen, was a little more orderly. All of his clothes and belongings were packed in boxes. A red trolley stood next to them. His bathtub was ringed with grime. Inside the medicine chest I found a bottle of Lipitor, some aspirin, and antacid. As I walked back into the bedroom, I noticed half a sleeve of saltine crackers and a can of Lipton iced tea with a straw in it on his nightstand. I assumed he had both a heart and a stomach condition.

"Mom, how are you holding up?" I asked.

"Barely," she said.

"Do you want to wait in the car while I finish looking around?"

She shook her head and walked back into the living room. I stayed in the bedroom. I stared at those saltines; they were probably his last meal. I noticed that the impression of his body where he last slept was still visible on the bed—if he'd managed to sleep.

I knew what had happened here, but the question was why?

In the living room, I remembered another line from Grissom: "There's always a clue."

I found a knife and opened one of the boxes in the bedroom. Soon I was ripping open all of the boxes. It wasn't proper CSI procedure, but screw it, I wasn't a real cop. I was a guy looking through his dead father's stuff, hoping to find a note or an explanation of why he had called it quits.

A short time later, I stood among a pile of Eddie's belongings—shirts, books, letters, knives, mementos from jobs, photos—everything he'd planned to take with him wherever he was going. I studied the pile. I assumed these were the things he needed or that meant something to him.

Then it hit me.

I hadn't found a single item with anything about me, nothing about *CSI*, nothing that indicated he'd followed my career, nothing that indicated he'd even thought about me.

This is what I'd feared back in my office—not Eddie's death as much as the life I was going to find, and apparently what I wasn't going to find.

I found myself wanting to know my dad. How strange. Emotions twisted in ways I didn't understand. Twenty-five years of basically no relationship, no acknowledgment of our connection, a DNA that stood for Dad Not Around, and all of a sudden I wanted to have a relationship with him. How was that possible?

I picked a helluva time to want to get to know him.

I was frozen in time and place. The best I could do was to ask myself questions that couldn't be answered—at least not immediately.

Had he ever thought about me? Did he regret not knowing me better? Not spending more time together when I was a kid? How about as an adult? Did he know about my connection to *CSI*? Was he a fan of the show?

The show had been on the air for five years. There were two spin-offs. It was on its way to being the most-watched show in the world. Yet he'd never called, sent a note, nothing. He hadn't even asked for money.

I repacked the boxes so I could take them home. I'd look through them and his other possessions again when I was calmer.

As I stood up from the last box, I looked at his TV. I realized it was directly across from the couch where he last sat. Could he have . . . ? No, no way. Then again—could he have seen me on TV the night before, picking up an award for *CSI* on the People's Choice Awards?

I switched on the TV to see the last channel he'd watched. It turned out to be the local CBS station. It was entirely possible that he'd seen me.

"Wow," I said under my breath.

My mom turned.

"How could he have done this to himself?" she asked.

I shook my head. I didn't have any answers—not yet. I remembered a line Marg Helgenberger's character, Catherine Willows, once said: "The thing that makes a fantasy great is the possibility it might come true. And when you lose that possibility, it just . . . kind of sucks."

Clearly, it did.

"How was it?" my wife asked.

I was with Jennifer, in the kitchen of our Vegas home. She put dinner on the table. I wasn't interested.

"It sucked," I said.

"And your mom?" she asked.

"It was tough. But as she said, it was tougher on Eddie."

I told her the CSIs had cleaned the place pretty thoroughly. They weren't able to remove the specter of failure and defeat. I described Eddie's living conditions, the dirty dishes, the grease, the scum in his bathtub, and all the boxes. I told her about finding a white pillow cinched with a belt and stained with blood. I wondered if he'd used it to muffle the sound of the blast. (Later, I found out he used it to rest his sore neck when he watched TV.)

"Did you take anything?" Jennifer asked.

I nodded.

"A lot," I said. "But probably not enough."

Indeed, I had returned home with boxes of his belongings and put them in my office. My haul included papers I'd scooped up from his table, bank records, his cell phone, and even paintings he'd done in the 1970s and

1980s. He had talent, and I suspected he might have ignored his creativity or channeled it in the wrong ways.

"Look at this," I said, pulling a half-dollar-size piece of bone from my pocket. "I remember this from when I was a kid."

"What is it?" Jennifer asked.

"A shark's tooth," I said. "My dad always had it. I don't know why, but it's one of those things I remember clearly."

After Jennifer went to bed, I ventured into the garage in order to confront all the things I'd taken from Eddie's apartment. Taking a deep breath, I surveyed the boxes, not quite thinking I was looking for a needle in a haystack but not quite sure what I was looking for, and not quite sure it was even in this stuff. Later, in fact, I would regret not loading everything in his place into a moving van. There was no rhyme or reason to what I did take, something I began to realize as I sorted things into piles. It felt like I'd made a last-minute sweep through his place, which, unfortunately, I had. It was a lot of stuff, but not enough. What did I need his VHS tapes for?

A CD caught my eye. Actually, the writing on it got my attention. The clear jewel case was labeled "Father and Son," and it stuck out from within the mess of stuff. I set it aside and made a mental note to play it later. I also pulled out some old issues of *Oui*, the '70s porn magazine that I remembered my dad used to have on his coffee table in his swinging heyday. That took me back in time. So did a few old watches and gold chains I found, as well as a set of small wooden boxes that once stored his coin collection.

Then I saw Eddie staring up at me. His Bank of America card was sitting there with his picture on it. I double-checked to make sure it was him. The man in the photo was older and bloated, not the slender, muscular, good-looking guy I remembered from my childhood. I had a hard time reconciling the change. The same was true with his bank statement, which I found beneath the card. He had fifty-five thousand dollars in his account, more than enough for him to get by.

As I went through his papers, though, I found an old AAA map of the United States. I unfolded it and saw a route from Las Vegas to Florida highlighted with a yellow marker. From some notes and bills of sale, I figured out he'd planned to move to Florida. Apparently, a few years earlier, he'd bought a plot of land and sold his condo, but then ran into some tough breaks, including Hurricane Katrina, which sent the price of motor homes soaring. Like so many of Eddie's schemes, his plan fell through, and he ended up in that apartment, defeated, depressed, and finally dead.

I stood up to stretch my back and heard myself against the backdrop of late night quiet taking deep breaths, as if I were lifting weights in the gym. I was lifting a different kind of weight, I supposed. After nearly two hours of searching, I had a good sense of my dad, and then I noticed a legal pad with notes on it. The lines were thick, as if someone had pressed down hard with a ballpoint pen. I immediately recognized Eddie's left-handed scrawl. The severe slant was just like mine.

Eddie had always been a ferocious letter writer. If he

felt wronged, he punched back hard and fast. Even on a few occasions when I got into trouble as a little kid in Catholic school, he wrote heated letters to the nuns. He didn't defend me as much as he took the opportunity to vent at them and their institution. He had opinions and issues, and both were woven so tightly they couldn't be separated. As I read his most recent epistle, I learned he was still letting out steam, although he seemed about done throwing punches.

"I have to get out of here," he wrote. *"I don't know what I'm going to do or where I'm going to go. Florida fell through. Life's hard and I've taken my share of knocks—that's for sure. The ocean's where I'd like to be. If I can live anywhere, it's not in this godforsaken desert town. I'm done here. There are too many ghosts, too many wrong turns. I've always liked the water. I can envision at the end whenever that comes being buried at sea. That would be my choice, though when I'm gone I don't know how much choice I'll have . . ."*

For the first time since I'd heard the news, I lost it.

I don't cry easily, and to be honest I didn't cry then, but inside I fell apart. I caved. Reading those words, I could hear my dad clearly. It was as if he was talking directly to me. It wasn't so much like we were suddenly all square as it was that I was sorry for the way things had turned out for him. He'd done me wrong so many times, but now, I realized, I had a chance to end on a good note by paying his bills, contacting the people in his life, and making sure Eddie left evened up.

I didn't know exactly what that meant or where it was going to take me, but I promised to try.

11

The next morning I drove to the police station to re-
trieve my dad's personal effects—whatever that meant. I
couldn't imagine what else was left. Nor did I know how
to go about this or anything else that followed, which was
ironic given all the police work I'd observed and written
about. Reality was definitely another deal. But the woman
behind the desk understood. She handed me a printout of
instructions on how to clean out the house of someone
who has just died. I was taken aback: It was a how-to list,
an honest-to-God menu, like you'd get in a build-your-
own-burger restaurant. I was going through it with interest when I heard someone call my name. I glanced up and
recognized a guy behind the counter who'd lived next
door to me years earlier. Now, apparently, he was a cop.

"I'm sorry about your father," he said.

He offered me a chair behind the counter, disappeared into the back, and returned with a check for one
hundred dollars. He explained it was the cash Eddie had
on him at the time of his death. He also gave me my dad's
wallet, credit cards, and two puny Smith & Wesson pis-
tols. I reached out to shake his hand, as if to say thanks. I
forgot this was his job.

Next stop: the county coroner's office. I knew the

forensic pathologist Dr. Gary Telgenhoff from when I'd researched the *CSI* pilot. He'd let me shadow him for a week and ask questions, and we became good friends. In his off-hours, he played heavy metal rock. When he heard I was there, he came out from the autopsy room and took me into the back. He shook his head when I asked to see the body.

"No, I can't let you," he said. "There's nothing to see. He's all gone."

"I want to," I told him. "One last time."

"No, you don't want that to be the last time."

Rather than argue, I thanked him for offering his phone number in case I had any questions. Outside, I called a friend who had recently buried his father after a long battle with cancer, and I asked him what I was supposed to do with my dad. He recommended the Palm Mortuary, one of the largest and oldest such businesses in Las Vegas.

"They do burials, cremations, whatever you want," he said. "They handle everything."

I picked up my mom, who insisted on going with me, and the two of us pulled up in front of a large, orange brick complex, which included a chapel and a structure in the back that I assumed was the crematorium. We walked into a showroom, where a salesman greeted us in the manner of a close friend offering comfort. He wore a dark suit and had hands as soft as his voice. I found it strangely nice. I accepted his sympathies for our loss and followed him into his office. Motioning me to sit in a chair, he offered a brochure, which I politely declined. I didn't want to shop. I was done with menus.

"How do you want to bury him?" he asked.

"What do you mean?" I asked.

"There are options," he said.

I understood.

"Cremation," I said. "We'd like the body cremated."

"Okay, come with me."

He showed me a cardboard box for $35, an oak box for $150, and several other upgrades.

"This is just for burning?" I asked.

He nodded.

"I'll take the cardboard box," I told him.

"Very good," he said. "Now, shall we look at urns?"

"That's what we'll keep him in—his ashes, right?" I asked.

He nodded.

"I want something good," I said, turning to my mom, who was stoic as we went through this process. "I'm going to get Eddie a nice place."

Outside, my mom and I were relieved to have taken care of Eddie, and we were quiet as I drove her home. Afterward, I took a long route back to my place and began reflecting on the questions I still had about Eddie, the questions I'd asked the day before, at night, and all day long—the questions I'd asked since hearing the news: What had happened to him? What had driven him to that point? What had his life been like the past twenty-five years? How had he ended up on the couch with a gun in his mouth while I was a success in Hollywood? Did he know about my shows? Did he care? Had our paths crossed one last time that fateful night?

I wanted to know. I felt like I had to know—or at least try.

I heard Grissom's voice again.

Let the evidence tell the story. The facts don't lie.

PART III

VEGAS, BABY

12

JANUARY 11, 2005

At home, I made myself a cup of coffee and took it into the garage, where I had left Eddie's belongings as if he'd been there himself, waiting for me to come back. *Still here?* I thought. I could almost feel Eddie nod a defiant yes as I stared at the half-empty boxes and the contents I'd separated into piles. *Where the hell else am I going to go? I'm dead. This is just . . . junk.*

I picked up his answering machine, plugged it in, and hit play. I heard myself breathe as the tape began to turn. I had brought a notepad with me, and I waited eagerly to hear what if anything was on the tape. The seconds of silence seemed like hours, and then I heard a series of messages that had me hanging on every word. They replayed the moments that led to the discovery of Eddie's lifeless body.

MESSAGE ONE (A MALE VOICE): Eddie, how are you doing? It's me. Where you been? Haven't heard from you lately. You're supposed to do brick work for us this morning. But you're not here. Hopefully we'll see you soon. We've got a lot of work, okay?

MESSAGE TWO (THE SAME GUY): Hey, Eddie, it's been about an hour since I called. I'm going to have to take you off the job now. Sorry, man.

MESSAGE THREE (A DIFFERENT MAN, OLDER): Hello, this is Mr. and Mrs. Nesbit, your neighbors. We haven't heard from you for a while. We're a little concerned. Just call back.

MESSAGE FOUR (THE SAME OLDER MAN): Hello, it's us again. The landlord is outside of our door, asking if we've seen you. He wants to come in. Can you pick up?

MESSAGE FIVE (A THIRD MALE): Eddie, it's your landlord. Please answer. Oh boy, I'm not getting a good feeling about this.

MESSAGE SIX (ANOTHER MALE): It's the Las Vegas Police Department. Are you there? Answer the door. Okay, we're coming in right now.

I looked at the notes on my pad and saw details starting to appear. Eddie had a heart condition and a bad stomach. He'd given up taking care of himself. His last gambit had gone bust. He hadn't been seen for a while. He was getting by doing manual labor, which was hard for me to imagine. I couldn't picture my dad laying bricks. He wasn't that kind of guy.

I tried listening to the messages on his cell phone, but I couldn't get in without a passcode. I did notice that he'd stored the numbers of his friends, about twenty of them. Starting with the A's, I called every one of them. If they weren't home, I left a message. I was blunt. Their friend Eddie Zuiker had committed suicide.

Those who answered got the same story, with additional details. I said, "He put a sawed-off shotgun in his mouth and pulled the trigger." Harsh? Yeah. But for some reason I wanted his friends to hear the truth, blunt and unfiltered. I had no idea if one of them might have felt a connection or a responsibility to him.

It didn't seem like they had. Three of those who answered were women, and after registering their surprise, they said I sounded just like Eddie. Only one person took the news hard. That was Jesse, apparently his best friend. After hearing the news, he made a noise as if he'd been hit in the gut. The air went out of him, and then he went silent.

"You still there?" I asked. "Are you all right?"

"It's a hard one, kid," he said. "I'm thinking about what you just told me. It's a hard one to picture. I don't want to think of Eddie like that."

Jesse invited me to his house. He said he wanted to talk about my dad and get a sense of Eddie's kid.

"We'll drink to your old man," he said. "I'll show you some pictures I have."

I had my own pictures to look at—the pictures in my head.

"No thanks," I said.

The truth was, I didn't want to get involved. I didn't know Jesse. I didn't know whether he was connected, whether he had a past, whether my dad owed him anything. Seeing him could've been nothing. Or it could've been complicated. It was easier to say no thanks.

The hardest part was telling my grandmother, who was my dad's adopted mother, and his sister, Gloria, who had MS. I hadn't seen them for years. I put the trip off until the afternoon. I kept asking myself what the right thing to do was, as if there were a debate. Finally I got in the car and drove across town.

Fifteen minutes later, I pulled up in front of their single-story stucco home. Before getting out of the car, I stared at the front door, trying to remember the last time I'd been there. I couldn't. My aunt's assistant let me in and showed me to the kitchen. My wheelchair-bound aunt Gloria was waiting there with my grandmother, who spent most days watching religious shows on television.

They stared at me with expressionless faces as I gave them the same details as everyone else. When I described Eddie putting the shotgun in his mouth, my grandmother reached for my aunt's hand. She looked down and shook her head. It came out that they hadn't been in regular contact with him either.

"Eddie left fifty-five thousand dollars," I told them. "You should have it."

They exchanged looks, but without conferring or offering a reason my grandmother said no thank you. I knew they could've used the money, so their refusal said a lot about their relationship with Eddie. Before leaving, I gave them several old photos I'd found at my dad's apartment. In them, my grandmother was young and my dad and his sister were children. They were holding hands and smiling. My dad used to push those kinds of pictures to the side whenever I asked about them. "I don't remember back that far," he'd say. But of course he remembered. My guess is that he didn't want to think about what had happened during the years in between, and now neither did my grandmother nor aunt.

I left the pictures on the kitchen table and said goodbye. I had a pretty good idea that was the last time I'd see them.

13

Show me someone who is able to leave their past. I wasn't—and neither was Eddie.

He was adopted at birth and raised in Chicago by his mother, a hairdresser, and his father, a technician with the phone company. They were a normal, loving, hard-working Italian couple. In their old home movies I remember seeing as a kid, Eddie always looked happy. He told few stories that indicated otherwise. His worst childhood complaint? Having to take violin lessons. "He had it good," my mom said.

But Eddie was one of those people who was unable to appreciate when he had it good. Nothing was ever good enough, ever right, ever the way he wanted it. You don't have to be a therapist to connect the dots back to his being adopted. That scar was permanent. He probably would've denied any effect, but he was haunted his entire life by the psychological wound of being handed over to another set of parents. He never got along with his father, and by his middle teens he was ready to leave home. He joined the Marines immediately after high school and came out two-plus years later a tough, cocky young man.

In photos from that time, he looked out at the world through squinty eyes reminiscent of James Dean's. His head was angled and his hair was thick and combed over. After the Marines, Eddie enrolled in beauty school and studied to be a hairstylist. It wasn't the obvious move, but it made perfect sense if you knew Eddie. He had a plan— there was always a plan. First, Eddie knew he could earn a living as a hairdresser. More important, it was a way to meet women. He wouldn't even have to go looking for them. They'd come to him.

However, instead of living out the fantasy that Warren Beatty would turn into the 1975 movie *Shampoo*, Eddie fell for another beauty school student—my mom, Diane. Only seventeen and recently graduated from high school, my mom was easily swept up by Eddie's self-confidence and grandiose dreams. They made a handsome couple, I have to admit—like a young Mickey Rourke and Kate Beckinsale.

Late one night they were driving through town in Eddie's Oldsmobile Toronado when he pulled over to the side and turned to my mom. My mom thought he wanted to talk about his plan to open a salon. Since finishing beauty school, he was constantly figuring out ways to raise money. In his mind, one salon was going to lead to others, and then fortune and the good life. He wanted to be somebody who mattered, and to have a good time along the way.

But instead of the usual number, Eddie pulled a dia-mond ring out of his jacket pocket and asked my mom to marry him. Surprised, she couldn't take her eyes off the ring as he slipped it on her finger. It fit perfectly—exactly the way she thought about him: a perfect fit. She accepted his proposal on one condition—he had to get permission from her parents. She was very close to her mother and father, and she wanted their blessing.

Eddie didn't protest, but privately, as my mother tells it, he was concerned. Her father was a former cop turned barber who made extra money as a bookie. Her mother was a homemaker. As Eddie knew all too well, they were conservative and leery of this older ex-Marine pushing their daughter too quickly into a serious relationship. Yet Eddie made his pitch at a family dinner, got the necessary approval, and soon after, married my mom in a small ceremony at the local courthouse.

They drove to Las Vegas for their honeymoon and stayed at the Aladdin hotel; my dad drank and gambled while my mom stayed in their room.

She was underage.

14

My parents got an apartment in Blue Island, a suburb at the edge of Cook County, Illinois, and worked in the same beauty shop in nearby Riverdale. My mom was talented, but Eddie was the show. He had that look-at-me flair. I can't imagine that he minded working in front of a mirror all day. About six months after their honeymoon, my mom found out she was pregnant. She was still only eighteen. As she later told me, she was "a baby having a baby," adding, "I wasn't even done growing up."

She worked the whole nine and a half months, right up to the morning of August 17, 1968, when she called the salon's owner to say she was in labor and wouldn't be coming in. Neither would Eddie. She should have gone to the hospital that morning or early that afternoon at the latest, but the weather was terrible. Rain came down in sheets and tornado warnings were flashed across the TV every fifteen minutes. Despite the worsening labor pains, my mom wanted to head for the basement, not the hospital, to wait until the weather cleared before having the baby.

Eddie knew better than his young bride. Taking her by the arm and grabbing the bag of clothes she had packed, he put her in the car and drove to St. Francis Hospital.

Within a couple of hours, I entered this world, weighing six pounds, six ounces, and measuring sixteen inches long. Later, after my nervous mom nursed me for the first time, she looked up at the RN and said, "He's so small. What do I do with him?"

She learned from her family. Her large Italian clan gathered for dinner every Sunday at her grandmother's house, and there, at the table, the women passed me around while offering my young mother generations' worth of advice, the same tips and tricks they had learned from their mothers and aunts. Although these get-togethers were part of my mom's family DNA, my dad tolerated them, as expected from someone who felt unwanted at the core. He sat at the table knowing this wasn't going to be his life.

He had a tough enough time with his own family. As an adoptee, Eddie always believed he wasn't wanted and that gave him the psyche of a lone shark in a great big ocean. Although he had a wife and a new baby, he didn't feel beholden to anyone but himself. He was out for Eddie.

A week before I was born, Chicago hosted the Democratic National Convention, and it was a disaster. Anti–Vietnam War protestors clashed with police, and violence ripped through the city's streets. TV reports showed crowds being teargassed, hippies being beaten, and stores getting looted. Unnerved and frightened by the violence and disruption to the status quo, my mom followed her instinct to burrow closer to her family, where she felt safe and secure. My dad was the opposite. To him, the rioting was an excuse to leave town, and he knew exactly where he wanted to go—Las Vegas.

From the day he and my mom left Vegas on their honeymoon, Eddie began thinking about how to move there. He loved the city. It spoke to him. It hummed all day and night. He identified not with the vacationers looking to turn a hundred bucks into two hundred but with the guys running the operation, the guys looking for much bigger scores.

Vegas was still like the Wild West back then, but there were the rules, and coming from Chicago, Eddie understood the way things worked. The casinos were controlled by the mob, and many of the men in charge, guys like Frank "Lefty" Rosenthal, were from his hometown. But as Eddie saw it, he'd been adopted, so who the hell knew where his hometown was. Vegas was as good as any—better, in fact.

My mom didn't want to leave her family. She had a baby and relied on the support she got from her mother, aunts, and other relatives. But Eddie's persistence wore her down. In 1970, he packed up the car and drove to Vegas, where he bought a mobile home and got a job as a timekeeper at the Stardust hotel. He punched hotel workers in and out of their shifts. He knew it was a crap job, but he was in the door.

Two months later, my mom and I joined him. She had just turned twenty-one, making her old enough to get a job in a casino. The timing of that was so impeccable it makes me think Eddie had it all figured out. She was hired right away as a change girl at the Stardust. Pretty women like my mom never had a problem finding work in Vegas; they had other problems. Stationed near the slot machines, she spent eight to ten hours a day making change and smiling politely as men ogled her in her skimpy dress and high heels.

Gamblers, drunks, and even her own bosses—especially her bosses—were able to say anything they wanted without fear of recourse. And she just had to smile through every kind of degradation. From the start, the work left her bruised inside. And physically, the heavy change belt she wore around her waist wrecked her back to the point where she was in constant pain. Knowing she couldn't afford to quit, she cried before every shift.

About six months later, after scouring the hotel for openings in other departments, she became the reservation girl for the Stardust's *Lido des Paris* show. It was an important position. She dealt with all the department chiefs, from the casino manager on down. All of them called with requests for their high rollers. Everyone wanted tickets and good tables, comps and the best waitresses. It was a political minefield, but she learned to manage all the different demands and temperaments, and developed her own acquaintances.

At Eddie's urging, she went to the casino manager and asked if there might be a more substantial position at the hotel for her husband, who worked as a timekeeper. Proof that knowing the right people helped, Eddie was moved into the casino's cage, where gradually he worked his way up to cage manager, which meant he handled all the money. Once he had his hands on the cash, there was no telling whom he got involved with or how much he skimmed. That was par for the course in Vegas at the time. Later, as a kid, I heard stories that he sometimes walked out of the hotel holding a lamp stuffed with as much as fifty thousand dollars.

Even if Eddie exaggerated his tales of Vegas in the old days, he was on the inside—exactly where he wanted to be.

15

JANUARY 13, 2005

Eddie's friend Jesse called me back to say he went by my dad's apartment on his own. He'd wanted to see for himself that my dad was really gone, as if my word weren't enough. Jesse mentioned that the little grill Eddie had kept in front of his door was gone. "Stolen," he said, spitting the word out with disgust, as if word had gotten out that Eddie killed himself, and with no one watching his place people came by and took the grill and everything else.

"Vultures," he said.

"I know," I said.

"I looked in the window," he said. "I couldn't see anything. The entire place was cleaned out."

It was true. I'd already closed up his apartment. There hadn't been much to do. I'd been in and out that morning. One thing: I'd figured out the yellow pickup parked in front had belonged to him. I found gloves and knee pads in the back. Those were a harsh find. As I held them in my hands, worn, chafed, dirty, I could practically feel my dad busting his ass in the hot sun for no money.

Goodwill picked up his clothes, pots and pans, and furniture, and then I went to lunch. When I returned, the place was ransacked. Everything was gone—the grill, his cordless phone (thank goodness I'd taken the answering machine tape out earlier), a tattered patio chair, even the hose that had been coiled in front. Seeing it all gone save for the musty, bloodstained carpet made me think of picked-over bones out in the desert.

Vultures.

16

When my mom and I flew into Vegas for the first time, my dad picked us up wearing bell-bottoms, a wife-beater shirt, and gold chains. He hadn't dressed like that in Chicago. My mom looked at him and asked, "What's with the clothes?" A few months later, he drove home from work in a brand-new Corvette. My mom, who was on her way to work, said, "What in God's name did you do? There's no way for us to get three people in there."

Somehow she got the Olds back. But then my dad bought a speedboat, which he named Steppenwolf, after the band that sang "Born to Be Wild." My mom had no doubt that Eddie had changed in Vegas. However, by then they'd bought a house and she thought it was better to look the other way, or not look at all, rather than know all of his endeavors. She hoped he might grow up and change again. It didn't happen. One night she came home from work and found the house full of Eddie's friends. He was supposed to be watching me. Instead he was partying with his pals. My mom waded through the people until she saw Eddie sitting on the coffee table, with a girl on his lap as he told a story. Her arm was wrapped around him. My mom stared until he felt the burn from across the room.

"What's going on here?" she said.

"I'm having a party," he said, shrugging her off with a callous laugh.

It took nearly a year for their relationship to unravel, but Eddie made it clear that night that he was no longer interested in being married. In 1971, they finally divorced, and my mom and I moved into a two-bedroom apartment. In order to afford the rent, my mom gave up her job at the *Lido* and began cocktail waitressing in the casino, where she could potentially earn more from tips. Without a car, though, she had to bum rides and take cabs to work. She had to walk a mile just to go to the grocery store, then trudge back with all the bags.

Eventually she saved enough money to buy a car, but it put us in a precarious situation where we lived day to day, juggling bills without any margin for unexpected expenses, and on occasion, if tips weren't good at work, falling behind. My mom never let on how close to the edge we lived, but I still remember the night we came home and couldn't get in the apartment. I was about four years old, and it was right before Christmas. A hard red plastic case covered the doorknob, preventing her from putting the key in and opening the door. We were locked out.

After trying to pull the case off, she kicked the door out of frustration, before marching to the manager's office. She pulled my hand, forcing me to break into a trot to keep up with her. The manager seemed to be expecting her. He explained that she was late on the rent.

"But it's my apartment!" she said.

"No, it's *my* apartment," he told her. "And you owe me two hundred dollars."

"What am I supposed to do?" she asked. "I have a child! You can see I have a child! Where are we supposed to go?"

"If you don't have the money," he said, "I don't know what you're going to do."

Trying not to cry, my mom turned away, took a step or two toward the car, and then faced off again with the manager.

"I have to get in," she cried. "I have a baby. It's freezing out here. I will get you your money, but let us in."

The manager finally relented. He opened the door and gave her two days to come up with the rent. She called her godmother in Chicago and asked for a loan. Her godmother refused. She wanted my mom to return home. Desperate, my mom borrowed the money from a girlfriend at the casino and worked double shifts to pay her back. She also stole from the food trays the coffee shop set aside for employee meals. It cut down on the grocery bill. Every little bit helped.

When my mom was unable to get a better station at work, she quit to look for another job, figuring she could do better—and she did. One of the big hotels hired her as a cocktail waitress in their casino. After eighteen months of serving drinks in the casino, my mom took over the cigarette concession. The girl who'd been running it quit to start her own business and tipped off my mom to the opening. It was a moneymaker compared with waitressing.

Now that I was of school age, she set her sights on getting me into the neighborhood's well-respected Catholic school, St. Viator's. She wanted me to have the best available education. However, during her interviews with the nuns, she admitted being divorced and employed as a cigarette girl at a casino, and a short time later I was denied admission.

Upset, she demanded an explanation from the nun in charge of St. Viator's. The nun did not mince words. She said that she disapproved of my mom's background and lifestyle. My mother ignored the insult and marched to the Catholic school across town, St. Anne. She explained the situation. The nuns there were apparently more open-minded. They let me in, and according to my mom, I loved school from day one.

My mom also enjoyed having some time to herself. Still in her midtwenties, she started developing her own crowd—she became friendly with musician Bill Withers, some of the Jackson 5 entourage, and other singers and dancers she'd met in the hotel. Every so often she invited some of her friends back to the apartment, where they'd have a few drinks, play records, and dance. She approached new friendships with caution, but eventually connected with David, a captain at the hotel's high-end restaurant.

David was sharp. He was always immaculately dressed, with perfectly manicured fingernails and a deep tan that enhanced his bleached blond hair, which was feathered and slicked back. One afternoon my mom took me to the restaurant to meet him. He shook my hand and sat us at a table in the corner while he disappeared into the kitchen. A moment later, he returned with a platter of cookies from the pastry chef. They tasted as good as they looked, and he immediately won my support.

My mom was pleased the introduction went well. From then on, their relationship progressed quickly. David began spending nights at our apartment, and soon they decided to shop for a house. Pragmatists, they thought it was a waste to pay rent on two apartments.

After finding a home they liked, they hit a roadblock. Their combined savings was less than half of the ten thousand dollars needed for the down payment. As they braced for disappointment, the seller gave them six months to come up with the money, which they managed with a few hundred to spare. From then on, saving became a habit. They got a ceramic piggy bank and put in twenty bucks apiece as often as possible. They always had a goal—a vacation, a car, a swimming pool. Every night I heard one of them ask, "Did you feed the pig?"

They also needed that safety net. Two days before Christmas, my mom's boss at the casino asked her to "go upstairs" with him. She knew exactly what that meant. He was well-known for telling cocktail waitresses to either go upstairs with him or look for another job. And as he knew, few women could afford to say no, including my mom, who was in the middle of her shift when he delivered his message.

It was a cruel piece of leverage just days before the holiday. But my mom didn't care. She removed her cigarette tray and said, "You can take this tray and shove it up your ass." Then she walked out. She knew that was the end of her job at the casino, and she was right. She was fired that night. David was terminated a few days later. The casino boss knew the two of them were a couple, and as punishment for my mom's refusal, he fired David as well. Since David was in the union, he appealed the termination—and won. He got his job back, but was put in a different restaurant, and in a lesser position, where he made less money.

There was no point in complaining. The boss closed the entire restaurant, firing David first, and then everyone else.

17

It wasn't lost on me that life wasn't fair. As a first grader, I was a smart, enthusiastic kid who compensated for the tough times at home with an eagerness to stand out, whether it was getting laughs from my classmates or praise from my teachers. When homework assignments were passed back, I looked for gold stars and bright stickers on top.

One day in class, we made gingerbread men from scratch, decorated them, and went outside to play while they baked. After recess we hurried back into the class to eat our cookies. The teacher handed everyone a cookie, except for me. I was the only one in the class who didn't get one. I asked the teacher where mine was. She professed to not know. While she searched for it, I watched my classmates eat their cookies. It was torture. Finally, the teacher announced that my cookie must have escaped, and she sent the class back outside to look for it.

This time when we returned to class she set my cookie in front of me. It was now cold and missing a leg. I assumed it had been dropped. Out of everyone's cookie, why had mine been the one mishandled? That really irritated me. However, as I began to eat it, I noticed that all my classmates were watching me. They'd finished their cookies. Mine was the only gingerbread man left. That was even better than the cookie itself. I realized what had earlier seemed like a stroke of bad luck had actually turned into an even better situation—in this case, making me the center of attention.

You never know. I began learning a lesson that would repeat itself many times and cause me to say to myself, "Gingerbread."

Around this same period, David found work as a waiter at Moby Dick, a local restaurant. It was a step or two down from being a captain at the hotel restaurant where he'd worked, but he had a realistic, practical attitude, and he was confident of his ability to work his way back up. My mom, meanwhile, went back to the Stardust, this time in the sports book. Lefty Rosenthal himself had set it up in 1976.

My dad was still at the hotel, having moved up the ranks, and occasionally their paths crossed—usually because Eddie was up to one of his hustles.

One morning when she came to work, Eddie walked in and said, "I need you to take a bet for me." He wanted to put ten thousand on the sixth race. When my mom asked which horse, he said something along the lines of "blank horse"—meaning she should leave the ticket blank and write in the winner after the race. For obvious reasons, she said, "Eddie, I can't do that."

"Just book it," he snapped.

Under pressure from Eddie, my mom left the horse's name blank and took Eddie's ten grand. Moments later, the name of the winning horse miraculously appeared on my dad's ticket and he walked out with sixty-five thousand dollars cash in a suitcase.

On the occasions when my mom and David pulled the same shifts, they tried to leave me with my dad. If he was free, they dropped me at his house, where I would watch TV while eavesdropping on phone conversations with his friends, which were better than anything I could possibly watch. He was always talking about Lefty Rosenthal and his chief lieutenant, Anthony Spilotro. As a gambler, Eddie had a fascination with both men, as did many in Vegas.

Rosenthal was the brains of the oddsmaking business, and Spilotro was the muscle. Their friendship and eventual falling-out was like a real-life Scorsese movie, and later, in fact, formed the basis for the film *Casino.*

Spilotro cast an especially large shadow over everyone who worked in a casino. His job was to keep those involved in the illegal activities in line and make sure the skim from the casinos got back to the mob. He had no qualms about making good on his threats to harm those who crossed him. My dad was on the periphery of this activity. He never got mixed up in any of Spilotro's business. He was one of numerous guys on the inside who managed to squeeze a little extra for himself. But he wasn't a gangster.

FBI agents regularly came in and out of the casino, periodically shutting it down to look over the books. According to my mom, those who were around the money found the tension an impossible drain. And if you weren't involved in the skim, you kept a vigilant eye out for those who were. After a couple of years, my mom finally tired of the grind, the pressure, and the characters, and quit the sports book in order to become a blackjack dealer.

She went to school for two months and was assigned the graveyard shift. With my mom and David both working nights, the household dynamic underwent a severe change. They often went to bed about the time I woke up to go to school. I was in fifth grade then.

In addition to learning how to prepare meals and clean my clothes, I poured through comic books (*KISS, Double Dinosaur, Sad Sack and the Sarge*) that I bought at a nearby 7-Eleven and invented sports games.

Depending on my mood, I turned my bedroom into a soccer field, a hockey rink, a football field, or a basketball court. All were sports that I could simulate with a wad of paper and two empty coffee cans on opposite sides of the room. I played for hours. I could almost see the players and hear the crowd. I was fortunate to have a lively imagination. It kept me occupied and in a positive frame of mind.

It wasn't always easy. Take the annual fifth-grade science projects. Although I knew it was coming, I still dreaded the day the teacher announced the assignment. I had multiple reasons. First, the kids whose parents could spend money on supplies always had the best projects, and second, the kids who had a parent at home who could help also did well. Those who had both were usually among the winners. And I wasn't in either of those groups.

Since winning, as I soon recognized, was beyond me, it was not among my concerns. My primary objective was to not embarrass myself. I didn't want to show up at school with a project that would billboard the fact I didn't have any help or any money. It was a science project, not a window into my home life. I didn't want to get a poor grade, either. But that was slightly less important than not making a fool of myself.

I walked home as if teetering on the edge of a cliff. I went into the garage and scanned the shelves and boxes for inspiration, something that would scream "science project." Nothing caught my attention, but in the course of looking around I got the idea of making a glacier. The whole thing flashed in front of my eyes: the cold version of a volcano, which several classmates had announced they planned to make.

Once I thought of my clever twist on the science project staple, I practically burst with excitement and could hardly wait to start construction. My tools were simple: plaster of Paris, blue and white paint, glitter, a borrowed glue gun, and an old Fisher-Price toy for the base. I worked it all up, including crevice-like pockets that I filled with water. Then I stuck it in the freezer for three days before taking it to class, where I explained, "This is nature changing in front of our eyes. As it sits here today, you'll see parts melt and break off, like a real glacier."

My presentation seemed to go over well, and I was pleased with my execution. Then I sat at my desk while my classmates gave similar demonstrations of their efforts at illustrating science. I compared each one to my glacier, which sat on a shelf amid a growing pool of water that began dripping in narrow rivulets down the wall and onto the floor.

"Tony's project is making a mess," one girl said.

"It is not," I said. "It's melting. That's what glaciers do."

"I agree," the teacher said. "I'll get some paper towels."

After all of the presentations were made, the class went outside for recess, allowing the teacher to hand out prizes. I moved a bench beneath the classroom window, stepped up, and pressed my face against the thick glass window, putting my hands around my eyes for a clearer view inside. Amazingly, there was a blue first-place ribbon on my glacier.

"Yes!" I exclaimed.

I jumped off the bench, turned toward the playground, and pumped my fist in the air. I felt like running a lap around the yard. The glacier had been 100 percent my own effort, a claim few of the other kids could make.

At the bell, I raced back into the classroom to get a close-up view of the blue ribbon on my project. Instead I found it had been placed on someone else's project. Angry and confused, I looked for the teacher. She was across the room, congratulating the new winner, a girl with an elaborate presentation about the water table and precipitation in the desert. Her chart could have been used in a lecture to graduate students.

My teacher put her hand on my back and steered me to a quiet corner where everything spilled out of me all at once—what I'd seen through the window, questions about why it had been moved, tears, and a final cry of outrage: "It's not fair!" She put a finger up to her lips, signaling me to stop. I expected an explanation to follow. It didn't. Instead she said, "Everyone here is a winner. Now sit back down, Tony, and let me get back to the lesson."

I was incensed. The nuns spoke endlessly about honesty and a sense of fair play, yet this was blatant hypocrisy. I wasn't being told the truth. I had seen the first-place ribbon on my project, then it was moved and my teacher had avoided providing a reason why. Though I had no recourse in the classroom, I vowed to make myself a success to show them how wrong they were. It was a defining moment in my life. I didn't care what I had to do. Those nuns would see I was a blue-ribbon kid.

My mom endured a similar injustice. After nine months at the Stardust, she'd lost her job dealing 21. A new regime had taken over and they brought in their own people.

"That's not fair," I said.

"I know," she told me. "But that's life."

18

For seventh grade, I transferred to Woodbury Junior High, a public school. Compared with St. Anne, it was enormous. Everything about it was bigger: the building, the number of students, and the athletic facilities, including a large, grassy field where I was able to play soccer, which hadn't been available at my previous school. I was a phenom on the field, with impressive speed and a knack for stitching the ball through crowds and into the goal.

The classes themselves were easier and I was relieved to be around many other kids whose parents weren't wealthy. Few had attended private or parochial school, and they had no idea how lucky I thought they were to be in class without fear of a nun slapping their hands for one infraction or another. But I had too much freedom all at once and my grades plummeted.

My first-semester report card included a C, a D, and an F in science. My mom had a fit when she saw those grades. After pushing to get me into good Catholic schools and always emphasizing the importance of education, she expected better from me. I made up a sorry excuse about my poor marks and swore that I'd do better. It didn't matter to her. She was too upset. She called my dad and then without any explanation simply said, "Here, Tony will tell you about the grades he just brought home."

Minutes later, my dad's Monte Carlo screeched to a stop in our driveway. He stormed in, grabbed my arm, and swung me into a kitchen chair. "I'll tell you what, sport," he said. "The next time you get an F, I'm going to take a pair of scissors and cut the word *soccer* out of your dictionary and make you eat it. Then I'm going to beat the shit out of you."

I bit my upper lip, petrified he was going to give me a preview of that beating. I was also trying not to cry. I knew that would elicit a bad reaction, too.

"Do you hear me, son?" he asked.

I nodded.

"Good—trust me, we do *not* want to be having this conversation ever again."

Fear was an excellent motivator. I applied myself with a new vigor. The library became my favorite place, my new home away from home. After finishing my work, I read the encyclopedia for pleasure. I leafed through magazines. I gobbled up facts and information and tried to work them into classroom discussions. Sometimes I was successful, other times I missed the mark. But one of my teachers, Mr. Marvin, noticed my effort and went out of his way to offer encouragement.

"Tony, you have the potential to distinguish yourself," he said one day as we walked past the ninth-grade lockers to class. "You're one of those kids who can be a success in anything you want if you keep your head screwed on."

I was eager to live up to expectations, and my next report card was filled with A's and A-minuses. It was a complete turnaround, and I kept it up. I watched proudly as my mom put a sticker on the back of her car that said "My Son's an Honor Student at Woodbury Jr. High." Afterward, she put me on the phone with my dad.

"I'm glad I didn't have to beat your ass," he said.

I was, too.

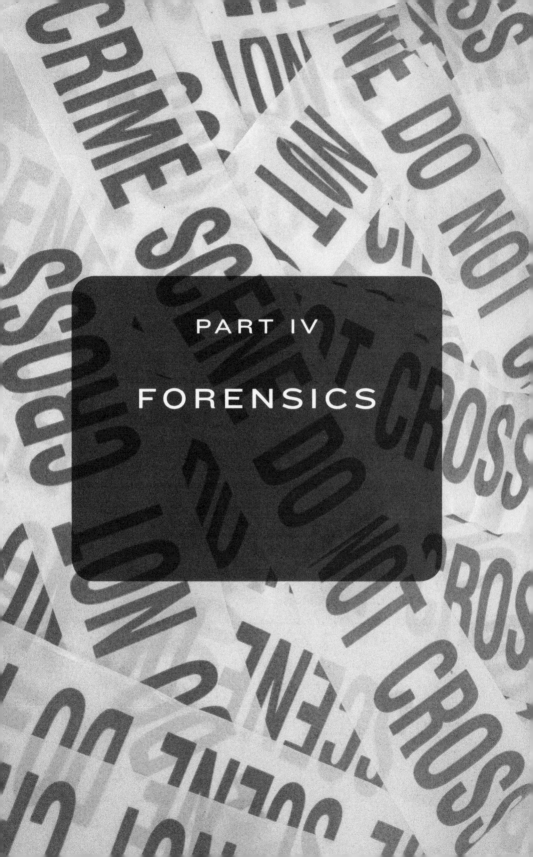

PART IV

FORENSICS

19

JANUARY 14, 2005

It was sunny when I walked out of the Palm Mortuary with the marble urn containing my dad. A few minutes earlier, the salesman who had helped me had presented it to me with a solemn nod, saying, "Here you are, Mr. Zuiker." My first thought had been to ask, "Which Mr. Zuiker are you speaking to?"

I didn't.

I thanked him and walked outside, where the sun hit me straight on. I stopped and put the urn down so I could fish out my sunglasses.

"Just a minute, Dad," I said.

As I picked up the urn again, I realized it was heavy. On my way to the parking lot, I gave in to curiosity and tried to open it. I wanted to see the ashes.

I couldn't, though. It was sealed.

"I guess you're stuck in there," I told him.

Once I got to my car, I debated whether to put the urn in the trunk or the front seat. Was there protocol here? A law? The trunk didn't seem right. Although it was heavy enough that it wouldn't bounce around, I still worried and thought there was something creepy, and so not-me, about driving around with a dead person in the trunk. I opened the passenger door and laid the urn on the seat.

"Dad, you're riding shotgun today," I said, not thinking of the irony.

Instead of going straight home, I stopped at his Bank of America branch. I needed to finish the paperwork required to transfer the fifty-five thousand dollars left in his account over to mine. Before getting out of the car, I looked at the urn and said, "I'll be right back." Instead, as I filled out the forms, I resisted the urge to run back out and check on my dad. With my imagination, I couldn't help but think, what if someone broke into the car and took the urn?

"Still here?" I said, getting back in the car.

It was strange. I hadn't really spoken to Eddie for more than a quarter of a century and now I couldn't stop.

"It's a helluva time to get reacquainted, don't you think?" I said.

I thought back to his apartment: the sofa, the belted pillow for his sore neck, the dishes, the saltines by his bed, the sawed-off shotgun . . . and now, three and a half days later, he was beside me, ashes in a marble urn.

"Eddie, what happened, man? How'd it get that bad?"

I pulled out of the parking lot. Suddenly I wanted to see some of his old haunts, not that any were still there.

"How about a drive, Eddie?"

In the silence of what would've been his turn to respond, I remembered the CD I'd taken from his place. It was in my jacket pocket. I reached into the backseat, felt around in my jacket, and pulled out the disc, which was marked "Father and Son." I studied it hesitantly, curious about what might be on it, almost feeling frightened but not really. Would it offer a clue as to how my dad felt about me? Or whether he thought about me at all? It was such a curious choice of title.

Screw it.

I pushed the disc into the CD player. A second later, I heard the scratchy sound of empty air, then the strum of a guitar—two chords, repeated three times, followed by the plaintive voice of Cat Stevens singing the opening words to his song "Father and Son." Although not deeply familiar with it, I knew it was a classic from the seventies about a father and son trying to understand each other. It was such sentimental drivel. And yet.

"All right, I'll listen," I said.

I turned it up and glanced at the urn.

"We're passing the spot where the Leaning Tower of Pisa used to be," I continued. "Remember?"

The Leaning Tower of Pisa was Eddie's favorite restaurant because it was also Rosenthal's favorite hangout. They didn't know each other, of course, but both liked the bar there, Home Town. After that, I did the whole tour. I drove past Chateau Vegas, Piro's, and Tony Roma's, the rib joint on Eastern Sahara Boulevard where Rosenthal survived an assassination attempt in 1982. Eddie had also liked Battista's Hole in the Wall, an Italian joint popular with the Rat Pack in the sixties, as well as Gianni Russo's place, State Street.

The song ended, but by then I was deep in Memoryland, thinking about a time when I was about twelve years old and my mom and I stopped in at Nevada Bob's golf shop to buy a gift. As we walked down an aisle, she froze in her steps and without saying anything put a hand up, signaling me to stop, too.

"What?" I asked.

"Let's go," she said.

"What?" I asked. "What's wrong?"

"We're leaving."

In the car, she asked if I'd seen the large, dark-haired man by the register. I hadn't. She said it was Anthony Spilotro, and she didn't want to be anywhere near him. She didn't know if he had ties to Eddie through the Stardust and also somehow knew that she was connected to Eddie, too, but she didn't want to risk it. As far as she was concerned, those men were best seen in the newspaper when they were on trial or attending a funeral—preferably their own.

When I next saw my dad, I mentioned Spilotro's name and got a different reaction. We were at his place on Pearl Street, a large house with a near-Olympic-size swimming pool he kept heated to 90 degrees all year. A faint, knowing smile appeared on his face and he said, "Yeah, Spilotro." Nothing more needed to be said. By now, I knew all about Spilotro, and I thought of the most heinous of the stories I'd heard, the one about him squeezing a guy's head in a vise until his eyes popped out.

"What about him?" my dad asked.

I told him about being in Nevada Bob's. He nodded, grabbed a few sour cream and onion potato chips from a bowl he kept filled on the coffee table, and said he had to make a phone call. He walked outside on the patio, holding his phone, which was connected by an extra-long cord. Unsupervised, I slipped off the couch and onto one of the large pillows he had on the floor, taking with me one of the *Oui* magazines on the coffee table.

The first time I saw a woman naked was when I was Dumpster-diving with friends and came up with a bunch of Polaroids of nude women. I was seven or eight years old. The pictures were probably tests from a photographer doing porn. After finding them in my possession, my mom summoned my dad to handle the situation. He stuck them in his pocket, then left.

His parting words? "I'll take these."

Now, he probably wouldn't have cared if he'd seen me looking at his *Oui* magazines, but the explicit pictures seemed better viewed in private. He kept some joints out in the open, too. The details were important to him and the friends he invited over, especially the women. It was all part of his playboy lifestyle. He was part of Vegas. He was happening. He had cash—and flash.

By contrast, my mom and David lived frugally, paid the pig, and watched every dollar they spent. They wanted a swimming pool very badly, for instance, but with my mom still looking for a job and David still working his way up, they didn't have the ten thousand dollars it cost. Somehow the older couple who lived across the street, the Canfields, found out. They liked my mom and David, knew they struggled, and one afternoon they walked across the street with a bag of money, ten thousand in cash, and offered it to them as a loan.

Soon we had a really nice pool. My mom got hired as a dealer at the Imperial Palace and David was made the maître d' at Moby Dick, and eventually they paid back the Canfields. As they got back on track, my dad lost his high-paying job at the Stardust. A new crew came in and installed their own people, and he found himself out of work for the first time since moving to Vegas.

Thanks to his contacts, Eddie was able to move over to the MGM Grand, a twenty-six-story hotel with two thousand rooms. He managed the casino cage, and was eager to impress and expand his reputation inside this new operation. Early on the morning of November 21, 1980, however, an electrical short behind the refrigeration unit in one of the hotel's restaurants started a fire, which spread through the second-floor casino, filling the elevator shafts and airways with thick, black, toxic smoke.

When fire broke out at 7 a.m., an estimated five thousand people were already in the casino, including my dad. As soon as my mom heard the news, she raced over to the hotel to see if Eddie had made it out alive. In the end, eighty-five people were killed and 650 were injured. Amid the chaos of firefighters, ambulances, and panicked guests, though, she spotted Eddie, a wet bandana covering his face, hurrying out the side, with a strongbox full of cash in each hand. He put them in his car and drove off.

Around this time, the government brought its heavy hand down on organized crime's involvement in the casinos, including the skimming that was basically an institutionalized part of the system. The mob didn't go quietly. In 1981, there was an attempt on the life of Nevada Gaming Commission head Harry Reid, now a United States senator from Nevada. I still recall the local media showing police crime scene tape around the Stardust's cage. The message was clear: Vegas was going legit. Indeed, the mob was run out of town and corporations came in. Old-school guys like my dad were screwed.

But Eddie was optimistic. He had the cash from the MGM, untold additional assets he'd buried, and ideas for going legit himself.

20

When I started tenth grade at Chaparral High School, I set my sights on going to college. I carefully planned my schedule around the requirements, except for my elective, the one course left up to me. My choices included botany, government, art history, forensics, and shop. I picked forensics, thinking it was like *Quincy, M.E.*, the TV series starring Jack Klugman as a medical examiner who used forensic science to investigate murders.

On the first day, though, the teacher stood in front of the class of about thirty-five students and welcomed everyone to speech class, also known as *forensics*. My eyes widened with surprise. What class was I in? *Speech?* For a moment, I thought about raising my hand, explaining that I'd made a mistake, and might need to transfer. Then I noticed a bunch of trophies around the classroom. They were from speech competitions. I liked competitions.

Intrigued, I raised my hand and asked how the contests worked. After hearing the teacher describe a typical tournament, with its different categories, I saw these were based on intellect, creativity, and skill—and I decided to stay in the class. Like many of the students who had signed up, I sensed it would help hone skills I'd need to succeed in college and beyond, including reading, writing, and public speaking. Maybe I could even get a trophy along the way, too.

A few weeks into the class, the teacher had some of her more experienced juniors and seniors perform their interpretations of speeches and poems. I was especially impressed with the way one young woman—a state champion, it turned out—performed a poem. The poem itself impressed me. It was an epic story, not a simple rhyme, and for some reason hearing it read like that made me want to know more. In fact, it made me wonder if I could do the same thing.

After class, the teacher motioned to a shelf of literature available for competition. She instructed us to pick a piece that we could start to learn. I went straight to the poetry section. I looked through several books before picking a collection of American poems, and that night, after paging through the thick anthology, I chose Edgar Allan Poe's lyrical ode of ill-fated love, "Annabel Lee."

> *It was many and many a year ago,*
> *In a kingdom by the sea,*
> *That a maiden there lived whom you may know*
> *By the name of Annabel Lee;*
> *And this maiden she lived with no other thought*
> *Than to love and be loved by me.*
>
> *I was a child and she was a child,*
> *In this kingdom by the sea,*
> *But we loved with a love that was more than love,*
> *I and my Annabel Lee;*

With a love that the wingèd seraphs of heaven
  Coveted her and me.

And this was the reason that, long ago,
  In this kingdom by the sea,
A wind blew out of a cloud, chilling
  My beautiful Annabel Lee;
So that her highborn kinsmen came
  And bore her away from me,
To shut her up in a sepulchre
  In this kingdom by the sea.

The angels, not half so happy in heaven,
  Went envying her and me;
Yes! that was the reason (as all men know,
  In this kingdom by the sea)
That the wind came out of the cloud by night,
  Chilling and killing my Annabel Lee.

But our love it was stronger by far than the love
  Of those who were older than we,
  Of many far wiser than we;
And neither the angels in heaven above,
  Nor the demons down under the sea,
Can ever dissever my soul from the soul
  Of the beautiful Annabel Lee:

For the moon never beams without bringing me dreams
  Of the beautiful Annabel Lee;

ANTHONY E. ZUIKER

And the stars never rise, but I feel the bright eyes
  Of the beautiful Annabel Lee;
And so, all the night-tide, I lie down by the side
Of my darling—my darling—my life and my bride,
  In her sepulchre there by the sea,
  In her tomb by the sounding sea.

Discovering the poem, which I read over many times, awakened a fire in my youthful romantic soul. I confided to one of the girls in class that I thought "it was pretty great." When I practiced it at home, I recited it in the manner of young Richard Burton, applying thick layers of emotion to each line while modulating my voice to reflect the delicate twists in the story.

I thought I was good. But several of the juniors and seniors let me know it would probably be a smart idea for me to quit. They actually went out of their way to tell me that I was quite bad. It didn't make any difference—I was hooked. I liked the preparation—working up a piece, getting into the writer's head, planning the recitation, thinking about the audience's reaction, memorizing the work—as much as the performance itself, maybe more.

I also gave myself some leeway for being a novice. I knew my inexperience had been accentuated from following a junior who had taken second place at the last statewide competition. The comments I received were due in part to the pressure those in forensics put on each other to excel. Here, talent and ambition were taken for granted, and everyone was expected to work their ass off.

After the teacher announced the date of the first competition, she urged me to find another category besides poetry. It happened that I'd been impressed with one student's interpretation of a scene from Sam Shepard's play *True West*. He'd done different voices and given life to each character. It was as if he'd acted the play while standing still. I wanted to do that. It opened me up to the possibilities I could have with a dramatic or expository piece.

One of the problems that forensics would help with was that I didn't have a strong voice or a confident identity—not yet, anyway. I didn't know who I was. I wore my hair neat, high-top Nikes—that swoosh was definitely a big deal—Levi's that had to be frayed at the ends, and cool surfer shirts. I listened to the whole Zulu Nation rap thing. I also liked *Jaws*, *The Godfather*, and *Kramer vs. Kramer*.

Basically, I was all over the map. But I sensed that, even though I was terrible at poetry, I was as good as, if not better than, the others in the class. I just needed to find a rhythm and get into it, something that worked for me.

We had another competition coming up and everyone in the class was scheduled to participate. This time, I chose expository speech, a style I thought was more suited to my personality. As for a subject, I chose Dungeons & Dragons, one of my favorite games, something I could talk about with authority and humor. I decided to make visuals, too.

I was hard at work the night before the competition when my dad stopped by the house, looking for my mom. He didn't say why he wanted to see her. Perhaps he was experiencing a moment of paternal interest but didn't know how to articulate those feelings since they were so rare and unnatural to him. Both my mom and David were at work. Eddie stood there, like a model in his jeans and a shirt that was unbuttoned to show off his tanned chest and gold chains. I told him that I was preparing for a speech competition the next day.

"Speech competition, eh?"

"Yeah," I said. "I'm doing expository."

I had a poster in my hand, one of the visuals I was still working on. I showed it to him, explaining that it was part of my performance. I still had to make a few more. Everything had to be perfect, I said. It was my first speech competition. He nodded, taking it all in. Then he cracked a smile.

"Expository," he said. "Isn't that something you shove up your ass?"

He laughed at his own joke. I was used to his crass sense of humor.

"It's a type of speech," I said. "About a specific thing."

I explained that I'd given a version of this presentation in class and received notes from my teacher. She'd offered encouragement, but said I needed to polish it further.

"Do you need any help?" he asked.

Help? From my dad? Whoa, that sounded like some weird parallel universe.

"Sure," I said. "I'd love some help."

"I'll tell you what. I'll pick you up at six tonight. I'll make sloppy Joes, and we'll work on your speech."

"All right," I said. "Cool."

A few minutes before six, I gathered my materials and sat on the front doorstep, waiting for my dad. I wanted to be ready. Six o'clock came and went, though, without any sign of him. So did six fifteen, and then six thirty. I waited until seven before going back inside. He never showed up, never called, never apologized. Devastated, I went to school the next day unprepared and screwed up at the competition.

Everything conspired against me. I followed two kids who nailed their presentations, my voice trembled as I began to talk, and while I was introducing my first visual, all the other drawings fell. Then, as I bent down to pick them up, the easel holding them up crashed to the ground. Laughter filled the front of the hall. I didn't look up after that. I was done—and I'd spoken for only twenty seconds. I still had another nine and a half minutes to fill.

When my teacher found out what had happened, she consoled me with a pep talk and suggested that next time I should utilize my humor. What humor? My eyes were red and filled with tears that I prayed wouldn't come out. She said I was funny, though, which I knew, and which also made me feel good. Did she also say there would be a next time? After two enormous failures, I thought I was finished.

"Tony, you have an ability," she said. "You're clever, you're funny, and you're smart."

"But I messed up both times."

"That's what happens when you're learning how to

do something," she said. "Could you ride a bike the first time you got on?"

I shook my head no.

"Tony, listen to me," she said. "You're a good kid. You're smart. You're going to get better. And you know what? If you work hard, if you really want to get good at this, I think you can be one of the best."

No one had ever given me that kind of encouragement. Deep down, I believed her.

21

For the next forensics competition, I wrote a speech about the Nerf ball, the foam toy that was billed as the "world's first indoor ball." I owned a Nerf, and I used it constantly. I played full-court basketball with empty Folgers coffee cans set against my bedroom door and the opposite wall. I used index cards to identify the two teams, North Carolina and Marquette, or whichever teams were playing in the week's biggest game. I was the players, the announcer, and the crowd.

I thought making it the subject of my speech was an inspired choice that would show off my sense of humor. But really, I was just writing about what I loved. All I knew about the Nerf was that it stood for "Non-Expanding Recreational Foam." That was it. In the day long before Google searches, you didn't have scads of information and trivia instantaneously at your fingertips. If I couldn't find it in the *Encyclopaedia Britannica*, I was out of luck.

Which was the case with the Nerf ball. So I made up my own facts about it. The speech was like a ten-minute comedy routine, starting with the variations of Nerf balls; there was the standard ball, the basketball, and the Nerf football. Why was it revolutionary? Because you could play with it indoors without, as the advertisements noted, damaging lamps, windows, babies, or old people, though I did mention an exception: a ninety-six-year-old woman who'd been killed playing Nerf football.

However, I quickly noted that I'd looked into that claim and found that she had actually died from being tackled by her 105-year-old husband. The message? Keep playing with your Nerf, but no tackling indoors.

For generations, I said, and in fact for as long as anyone could remember, children had been told not to throw a ball in the house. Now, thanks to the Nerf, they could. Was this progress or merely an attempt to subvert authority at home? I wrapped up my presentation by concluding that the Nerf was for children—and the naughty child in all adults.

I thought it was brilliant, clever, funny, and totally me. I had created several characters, which gave me the chance to do voices. By the time I finished, it was a piece I wanted to perform. I couldn't wait. I worked on it every day, practicing it over and over in front of my bathroom mirror, editing, adding, and most of all, memorizing. I was often still up at 3 a.m. when my mom and David came home and I performed it for them.

My mom had a large video camera, one of the earliest models, which I set up in the kitchen as the competition drew near. Before I could practice on tape, though, I had to write out my speech. And I wrote and rewrote it by hand, all fifteen pages, because even then I was someone who had to do it perfectly on the page or else start over again. It took me days to complete.

But finally the speech all came together. It was written, memorized, and practiced down to the smallest voice inflection and hand gesture. I even knew when to roll my eyes to get a laugh. I was ready.

With all the work I had done to make sure I didn't embarrass myself again, I'd failed to pay attention to the fact that the competition was, in fact, a county tournament, one of the biggest events of the season. I was aware of it, of course, but so deeply involved in my own preparation that I was oblivious to the pressures the others felt. They were there to sprint; I just didn't want to trip. But that worked to my advantage. With no one expecting much from me, I marched confidently to the center of the high school stage and performed my speech exactly as I had in front of my bathroom mirror, maybe better.

At one point, I saw my teacher laughing. As I wrapped up, I could feel the audience following me, and I left to healthy applause.

When the results were posted, I saw that I had *broken*, which meant that of the fifty expository competitors, I'd placed in the final six and advanced to the next round. In the finals, I felt the crowd with me again, used that groundswell of support to my advantage, and, as bizarre as it sounds, left the stage thinking I had a shot at winning it all.

In reality, there was no way that was going to happen. After lunch, teachers representing the different schools announced the six finalists in each category, including the winner. I was awarded second place and given a large gold trophy, which I clutched with a fierce grip lest anyone decide at the last minute that they had made a mistake.

When I got home, I walked in the front door with the trophy held over my head, hoping for a celebration. Unfortunately, that would have to wait. My mom and David were still at work. I didn't let the empty house deter my sense of triumph, though. I took five dollars from the pig and walked with my trophy to Wendy's, where I bought a burger and fries, a cup of chili, and a Frosty.

I savored every bite, but not nearly as much as I did seeing each person who passed the table glance at my trophy. Though I have a feeling that what they really noticed was my smile.

22

I continued with forensics as a junior, but switched from expository to dramatic interpretation. A talented senior named Christian Fisher had mesmerized judges all year and eventually won a championship with a monologue from Thomas Gibbons's 1980 play *The Exhibition: Scenes from the Life of John Merrick*, and once he graduated I took over the piece, hoping for similar results.

I mimicked Christian's performance, not quite as well but with a similar dramatic intensity, including the way I began with my back to the audience and slowly turned, explaining, "I wasn't always like this." I think Christian might have drawn inspiration from David Bowie's star turn in *The Elephant Man* on Broadway. My performance was probably closer to Audrey Hepburn.

But it was such a strong piece, and I sold it with the intense passion of a naïve eleventh grader falling in love for the first time with emotional literature, unafraid to show everything I felt. I'd lost any inhibitions I had about being onstage and spent my ten minutes in the spotlight transforming myself into John Merrick. My best friends on the team, Dustin Abraham and Rico Longo, told me I was great, and who knows, maybe I was.

I broke regularly in competitions, taking home

second- and third-place trophies and medals; by the end of the season, I made it to the district championship. My self-confidence soared. The winners of that competition would go to the nationals in Wisconsin.

Showing no signs of pressure, I advanced through the four preliminary rounds and broke into the quarterfinals, a group of twenty-four competitors. After the quarters, in which I gave my strongest performance yet, the school's theater coach, Mr. Johns, took me aside. He'd seen my scores in the prelims and quarters.

"How were they?" I asked.

"You got a couple of fives and fours," he said, noting some low scores. "But I know you made the finals."

"Yes!"

"But you're going to have to *picket fence* to get to the nationals," he warned.

Mr. Johns was trying to help, but there were reasons teachers weren't supposed to tell students their scores, as well as rules, and they were for moments like this one. A "picket fence" meant a one from every judge. One was the highest score, and it was nearly impossible to picket fence. Mr. Johns was trying to help, but telling me that I needed a perfect score was not exactly settling advice.

For some reason, though, it had the opposite effect on me. Instead of making me nervous, I grew more focused and relaxed. Having made it this far, I saw no reason I couldn't ace the final round, and after a deep, head-clearing breath, I gave my strongest performance yet. My scores were all ones, with the exception of a six. Since they dropped the high and the low scores, I got my picket fence and earned a spot in the nationals in Eau Claire, Wisconsin.

But the thousand dollars it cost to make the trip was out of our reach. At my mom's urging, I wrote a letter to Ralph Engelstad, the owner of the Imperial Palace, asking him to sponsor my trip. We never heard back. But I scrounged up the funds from various sources, including Eddie. However, once in Eau Claire, the trip was a series of errors. I burned the pants of my new Kmart suit trying to iron them, then got poison ivy from screwing around with a Nerf ball in back of the hotel, and within a round or two of the prelims I was knocked out. By comparison, my teammate Joey Slotnick—who would become a successful actor—got to the quarters doing Neil Simon's *Brighton Beach Memoirs*. He was sensational. I rooted for him from the corner, and saw what it took to compete at that level—and I wasn't ready.

But I returned home having seen what it took to win: preparation, research, talent, hard work, a break or two, and the self-confidence that it would happen if you applied yourself. I knew I had that in me.

23

One look at my dad and I knew he was up to something.
It was a Saturday afternoon, and I'd gone to his house
to hang out. He was "meeting" with a couple of young
women about his latest business venture, a modeling
agency. He called it Moonshadow Impressions. He introduced me to the women and explained they were models.
He told them that I was his son, Tony—and then with a
wink added that I was his "model consultant."

Later, he printed up business cards, including one for
me with that title: Tony Zuiker, Model Consultant.

Before I could do any consulting, the business folded.
He didn't know anything about running a modeling
agency. It had been a ruse to meet women, one of those
ideas that sounded great after a couple drinks with his
friends. But reality was his Achilles' heel.

After closing it down, he launched a line of perfumes.
He did it from scratch. Maybe he read a how-to book. I
don't know. But he threw himself into it. He ordered bottles, labels, and roll balls. And he named it Moonshadow
Impressions. Why let a good name go to waste, right?

One day I went over to his place and he asked me to
give him an opinion on several scents, including one he
called "Huntress." Suddenly I was his perfume consul-

tant. He sprayed them on my arm and stood back while I smelled each one. I thought all of them were nice. I also admired the logos. To me, they looked—and smelled—like sexy perfume.

Eddie looked pleased. He spread his arms, as if envisioning Moonshadow spreading across the globe, and told me his plan of putting the perfume in hotel gift shops, where tourists would snap them up and take them home as reminders of their hot Vegas vacation.

He launched it with a TV commercial featuring a beautiful woman in a skimpy cocktail dress (picture her alone on-screen against a black backdrop, a wind machine off-camera and cheesy electronic music providing atmosphere) purring about Moonshadow in a voice that let you know she was turned on and ready for a sexy night: "Hey everybody, can you feel it?"

It ran during *Saturday Night Live*. I was watching it at a friend's house with a bunch of guys, and the commercial came on between the monologue and Mr. Bill. I went nuts. "That's my dad's!" I said. "That's my dad's perfume!" My friends thought the woman was hot and cracked all sorts of jokes about what her Moonshadow made them want to feel. "Yeah, I can feel it," one of them said.

Two months later, he went bankrupt.

When I visited Eddie one weekend, all the Moonshadow bags and bottles were in the garbage. Soon after that he lost his house.

PART V

FINDING MY
VOICE

24

JANUARY 16, 2005

I had to get Eddie home, which meant it was going to be an unusual afternoon for the both of us. It had been a week since I'd arrived in Vegas to deal with the aftermath of his suicide, but it was time to get back to LA. Before leaving, I left a message for my mom, who was at work, and then chatted with my wife, who was about to take the boys to the pediatrician. After we hugged, I grabbed my bags and headed for the car waiting to take me to the airport. As I reached the door, Jennifer shouted for me to stop.

"Aren't you forgetting something—or someone?" she asked.

"Oh my God," I said.

I hurried back inside and picked up the urn containing my dad. Glancing at Jennifer, I shrugged, as if to say, "Nobody's perfect." Soon I was at McCarran International Airport, waiting in the security line. I wondered if there were laws about declaring what I had in the urn, which was now placed in a heavy cardboard box. As I'd quipped to a friend earlier, both of us were packed for the trip. The jokes were my way of dealing with nerves. I'd never traveled with a dead person before, and the last time I'd taken a trip with my dad had been a disaster.

This time was different. I made it through security without a problem, but then faced a new set of questions once on board the plane. Did I put him in the seat next to me? Did I put him in the overhead compartment? Would he rattle around? What if by some chance the urn opened up and he spilled out?

That settled it. I got to the gate and bought him a seat for the one-hour flight to Burbank.

"You're sitting next to me," I said.

Our last trip together, when I was sixteen, had ended our relationship. I couldn't help but think back to that time. After the failure of Moonshadow, he moved into a smaller house with his girlfriend, Brenda. He left her there when he and a friend went to Aruba to open a hotel and casino. His partner was a guy from his days at the Stardust, the son of a prominent casino boss. Like my dad, he had lots of schemes but little traction.

The Aruba plan was different only in that it was more audacious than all the previous ones combined, and both men were lucky not to get killed in the process. As I recall, it happened very fast. There wasn't much discussion despite the fact that such an undertaking requires detailed planning. You don't just decide to build a hotel and casino one day and then do it the following week. But that's about what it was like with Eddie and his partner. They were in Aruba for more than year.

During that time, I got my first job (at McDonald's),

bought a car (a convertible Beetle), and dated a nice green-eyed Greek girl (Zoé Karazaferis). On the surface, I was a normal teenager. But my dedication to schoolwork was anything but normal. I studied with a rage to succeed. The nuns who had cheated me out of my blue ribbon and my dad's threats were never far from my thoughts. I knew getting into a good college was a first step toward a prosperous career, and I wanted that very badly. I thought about it daily—more often than I thought about Eddie.

Every few months, he checked in with my mom, but his progress reports were more like reminders that he was still alive. According to him, work was hampered by riots, shootings, vandalism, corruption, and cultural differences. He claimed that the men on his crew pounded nails with the wooden end of the hammer. One guy stole my dad's underwear; he literally showed up with Eddie's purple Hanes sticking above his shorts. (Later, I saw a photo.)

To stay afloat, Eddie sold marijuana on the side—that is, until the authorities in Aruba stormed his place and almost killed him in cold blood. The whole thing was a farce.

One afternoon he materialized without notice in our kitchen. He wore a bandana on his head, and had a long, mangy beard and a deep tan. I actually thought he looked pretty studly, like a pirate. My mom had a different take; she cried. Eddie took a deep, painful breath as he looked away, almost with a wince. Seeing me, he pulled out a T-shirt from a backpack by his feet and flipped it to me. I opened it up. On the front, it said ARUBA SUCKS.

Something had happened there, something he didn't

or couldn't bring himself to explain, something that changed him. Looking back, it's pretty apparent. He had placed his last big bet on that hotel and lost. There was no telling whom he owed, just as there was no denying the life he had built over the years was slipping away from him, like sand in a timer, and he knew it, without knowing what to do next.

Then Eddie slipped out of sight. I didn't see him or hear much about him. I have a recollection of David and my mom talking about him in hushed voices. Whatever happened, they didn't think I needed to know. I supposed he pissed off the wrong people. Something along those lines. The next thing I heard, Eddie and Brenda had moved to Biloxi, Mississippi, her hometown.

I figured he was hiding out. It was too bizarre to imagine Eddie going that backwoods without a reason.

He flew me there once for a weekend visit. On that first night we stayed in a motel, but the next day he had to do a little bit of work where he lived. Seeing the confused look that put on my face, he prepared me for his living situation, explaining he was there on the QT. Everything Eddie had ever done, as far as I could remember, was always on the QT. Why should this be different?

I understood when we turned down the long, gravel driveway of a classic southern estate. Once through the front gate, I saw an enormous house with a pillared front porch surrounded by several acres of manicured lawn, giant trees, and flower gardens. I was still trying to figure out how Eddie had landed this sweet setup when he drove

past the main house and kept going until we got to a structure at the back end of the property.

Inside, Eddie turned on the overhead light. He was
quiet as I looked around and realized this was ostensibly
a toolshed. There were shovels and hoes leaning against
one wall, a tractor for mowing the lawn, and a tool bench.
Eddie led me into an adjoining room with a cot and a
counter that had a sink, a hot plate, and a microwave oven.
He said Brenda's parents owned the estate and let him live
there for free in exchange for keeping the place up.

"Huh," I said, shocked that Eddie had gone from a
mansion to this, a shed in the back of someone's house. It
was pretty humble ground.

The next day he and a buddy took me fishing on a
little river that ran through the woods and swamp, near
some homes and out-of-the-way shacks. Besides the gear,
they brought a chest of beer, a bottle of whiskey, and began
drinking as soon as they started the outboard motor. I sat in
the bow, with my back half-turned, trying to ignore their
crude conversation about women. I prayed they wouldn't
turn on me. But no such luck. After we threw our lines
in, Eddie and his pal passed their bottle and talked while
keeping half an eye on me. I'd never fished before. The
sun beat down, flies buzzed in the heavy Mississippi air,
and occasionally the water rippled on the surface as a fish
came up to eat. Then I broke the silence.

"Look at my line," I said.

My reel was bent at the end and the little float on my
line was bobbing up and down.

"I think I have a fish," I said. "Look at my bobber."

My dad turned to his pal and then laughed.

"What'd you say?" he asked.

"I think I have a fish."

"No. What else?"

"Look at my bobber," I said, pointing into the water. He laughed again.

"Did you hear the way Tony said *bobber*? Say it again. *Bobber.* Come on. *Bobber. Bobber. Bobber.*"

I was defenseless against such cruelty. Eddie's anger boiled to the surface the more he drank, and he aimed it at me. It got worse. On the way back, he pulled the boat up to crawfish traps that people had set on the sides of the river, pulled them up, and dumped those that were full into the boat. Laughing, he plucked the small ones from the pile and with a quick, backhanded flip of his wrist, smacked them against the large Evinrude motor. They made a popping sound as he killed them.

Pop! Pop! Pop!

I could barely look at him, yet I was afraid if I made too much of an effort to avert my eyes he'd get in my face again. On top of that, I feared some redneck would see him stealing from the traps and start shooting at us. I was waiting to hear gunfire. Later that night, we took the crawdads to his friends' house, a southern couple who whipped them into a delicious dinner, with new-skin potatoes and a pecan pie so sweet it made my teeth burn. But I wasn't able to enjoy it. I couldn't get past the fact that my dad had stolen the fish.

The next day, my last one there, he and Brenda took

me to the beach. After getting drunk and snorting cocaine out of a small amber-colored vial, my dad got in my face again. I could feel the heat of his inner rage as he asked if my mom had ever told me about the time he'd walked into the Riviera hotel with a shotgun, intending to blow her head off. Scared, I shook my head.

"Goddamn right she didn't tell you that," he said.

He took a swig of booze.

"Did she tell you that I never wanted you in the first place?" he asked. "Or were you able to figure that one out on your own?"

I tried to look strong even though I was petrified, but there was no pretending as he reached out and grabbed my shirt, ripping the skin underneath. He shook me hard, as if he wasn't sure whether to hit me or throw me to the ground. I'll never forget that look in his eyes. It was like staring into a furnace of burning rage. I didn't know if he hated himself or just despised me for having everything he'd lost: youth, ambition, and potential.

In the seconds he held me, in this ugly clash of manhood, I wanted to push him away, fight back, and cry, "Noooo!" Ultimately, I did nothing but stand there, in his clenches, until he let go and walked away, flailing his arms in disgust, as if to say, "The hell with you, and everything about you. I'm done." Instead he just walked over to his girlfriend. "Brenda," he said, "get me a beer."

I still hadn't moved or uttered a sound. I hadn't even wiped the tears that slid down my face. I just wanted to get the hell out of there.

25

When I got back home, my mom and David asked me how the trip had been. I responded with a curt "fine," and walked to my room. They realized something traumatic had happened. I had come back scarred. I kept my head down and was uncommunicative, which wasn't like me. I couldn't get past hearing my dad say that I was never wanted. Was he telling the truth? If not, why would he say such a thing to me? Wasn't he the one who'd been given up for adoption?

For days, I was a mess. Then finally I sat down at my desk with a pen and paper and wrote Eddie a long letter. I described each horrible, humiliating moment he'd subjected me to in Biloxi, along with an explanation of how intensely he had hurt me. I told him, in the plain type of language used on the playground, that I wasn't ever going to let that happen again.

"We're done," I wrote. "I don't want to ever see you again."

The new school year had just started when Eddie told my mom about the letter. He said he'd received it a few weeks earlier, at the end of the summer. I gathered he didn't share the details of either the letter or what had prompted it because when my mom came in my room to talk about it, she asked what I had written and why. Looking up from my desk, I told her that the trip had been pretty awful and I didn't want him in my life anymore. "Why, what did he tell you?" I asked.

"He said that he put your letter on file," she said.

I assumed "on file" meant that I was on his long list of people who had done him wrong. I thought he was pathetic for refusing to take responsibility for his actions and lashing out at me instead, but, as I'd made plain to him, I was done. I had nothing more to say. My mom saw enough of the pain and hurt in my eyes to understand all she had to. After a moment, she left me alone and I went back to my homework.

26

Although I didn't talk much about my dad, I opened up on occasion to the guys in my circle, especially my friend Dustin, who knew the situation for what it was and understood when it got to me. So did his father, Gary, who knew I looked up to him and responded with the kind of attention I craved when I was around him. He managed the city's largest Dean Witter branch, and he looked the part of an executive at a brokerage.

Through his job, he was in contact with Vegas's biggest players, including hotel mogul Steve Wynn, which impressed the hell out of me, as did his nice home, expensive car, and the spending money he was able to give Dustin. If he took his family out to dinner or the movies while I was at their house, he always included me. Likewise, if we were having a conversation and he thought Dustin and I were too flip, he laid into us—I received an equal part of the lecture.

When Gary talked to us about work habits, discipline, or responsibility—favorite topics of his when it came to dispensing advice—I responded positively. Dustin did, too. We had our obsessions with sports, rap music, TV, movies, and trying to persuade tired waitresses to slip us beers while we played parlay cards at crummy casinos that didn't care if we were underage. But we were also serious students, with a passion for speech class that superseded everything else.

Dustin was insanely talented. During my senior year, I began writing monologues for him. It was for our own amusement. He liked the way I wrote, and I loved seeing him perform my words. We were our own best cheerleaders. Then I wrote a piece he did in competition. Titled "HR-7," it told the story of abused children in a facility from the point of view of a kid who was paralyzed from the neck down but had all the answers inside him, so much potential, if only someone helped get it out of him, just like the Casio calculator that inspired its title.

It was a dark piece, and it took me years to realize it was as much a reinterpretation of *The Elephant Man* as a measured wail of my injured teenage soul pleading for a hug. When Dustin performed it, he put the audience in a trance; many were crying as he recited the litany of abuses he and the others suffered; at the end, they cheered as Dustin—battered, bloodied, but not beaten— vowed that nothing could ever stop him.

Dustin loved the monologue and was convinced I was going to be a famous writer. I hadn't really thought about writing professionally. Becoming a writer sounded good and glamorous, like a white-collar rapper. But I didn't know any writers. Nor did I know how to become one, though now it seems obvious—you simply write because you can't *not* write.

What I loved was Dustin's belief that I was going to be successful. I felt the same way about him. He planned on going to Hollywood to act. With his talent, I figured he was a sure bet. Along with our friend Rico, we also fantasized about becoming entrepreneurs. Our favorite rappers didn't just rap; they had their own labels and side businesses. They poured their cash into cars, furs, and jewelry. We wanted to own things, too.

I didn't want to wait until I was out of college to start making my fortune. I was too impatient. My head was full of get-rich-quick ideas, and I wasn't going to let the fact that I was a high school senior get in the way of making my first million dollars. Guys went into the NBA out of high school, so why not go straight into business? As I saw it, if I made millions, I'd be ahead of the game. If not, I'd have a portfolio I could take on future job interviews.

The first idea I had was to redesign an ad for Titleist golf balls that I'd seen in a magazine. I didn't know what to do with it once I finished, but I felt good about the effort. Next I made a leather belt with the waist sizes on the inside of every hole. I thought it was a genius idea. Who didn't want to know their exact waist size? I showed a prototype to the manager of the Gap at the mall. She held it in her hands, turned it back and forth, and then gave it back to me as if it were a dead snake.

"I don't get it?" she asked. "What's special about this belt?"

"You can see your exact waist size every day," I said. "You can know if you're getting bigger or smaller."

"You can know that without the numbers on the inside," she said.

"But with this belt, you know the numbers," I said. "Everybody wants to know their waist size."

"I don't," she said. "I'm going to pass."

I left the store convinced she had made the biggest mistake of her career. Although frustrated and disappointed, I was undeterred. I put the belt in my file and moved to my next great idea. I often chewed tobacco, and one day, as I tamped down my can of Skoal, I imagined a different kind of top that could be rotated to pack the tobacco tighter, making it easier to take a pinch, as well as keep the tobacco fresher. The user would also go through it quicker.

I sketched out a prototype and sent it to the US Tobacco Company. About ten days later, as I was doing homework, I received a call from a man who identified himself as one of the heads of product development for them. I braced for a life-changing conversation. In that moment, I thought, Okay, I'll forsake college for this million-dollar opportunity. But instead of praising my brilliance and asking for more ideas, the tobacco exec chewed me out for sending him an unsolicited idea. And I mean he chewed me out. He stopped a hair short of saying he was on his way over to kick my ass.

"I'm sending you a letter," he said. "It will have been vetted by our legal department and include the materials you sent us. They will be resealed. I suggest you destroy them."

"Sir," I said, shocked, "I'm only seventeen years old. I didn't mean anything by it. I just thought—"

"Son, I don't care what you thought," he interrupted.

"—it was a good idea you might want to buy."

"We don't *want* your ideas," he said. "Understand?"

"Yes, I do."

"Don't ever send anything to me again."

I didn't. But once again I bounced back. I made a greeting card with a picture of a tongue on the cover. When you opened it up, the tongue extended to reveal a special message: "I Love You" or "Hurry Back" or "I Miss You." (I envisioned a different message for every occasion.) Then, below the tongue, I wrote, "You took the words out of my mouth."

I sent the card to Hallmark's Kansas City headquarters. About two weeks later, a woman from Hallmark called the house, asking for Tony Zuiker. I braced for another lecture while secretly hoping she would say I was a brilliant new talent and offer me a career. I got something better—a nice person. After thanking me for the submission, she offered several comments and criticisms. I could tell she had taken a careful look at my work. Her manner was so positive that I expected her to say she wanted some changes but would buy my idea.

She didn't.

In the end, she turned it down, but with a sweet, caring sensitivity. She even said she was sorry to disappoint me. I assume she picked up on my age. She explained that many more cards were rejected than accepted when they came from outside the company. But she hoped it wouldn't deter me from future creative efforts.

DEC • 68

My father and me at Disneyland.

A Christmas
picture, Vegas
style. Eddie
with a cigarette
in his hand.

My late grandfather Louie "Papa Gay" Del
Nagro, grandmother Isabelle, Mom's brother
Louie, Eddie, Diane, and me as a toddler.

The science
project that
started all of my
rage as a child.

My first forensic
speaking trophy.
Second place at
county doing an
expository speech
on "the Nerf."

My seventh-grade soccer team, the Jets. My Mom would cheer *J-E-T-S, Jets! Go, fight, win!*

A college shot of me at Arizona State. I thought I was cool.

Writing The Runner at my mother's house. Notice the stickies on the wall.

Carol Mendelsohn and me on the set of *CSI* during the shoot of the pilot.

Billy and me on location in California. Bright and early. Science never sleeps.

My boys and me at the beach house in Malibu. My angels, Dawson, Evan, and Noah.

Speaking at the 250th-episode cake-cutting in front of
the cast and crew.

(COURTESY OF CBS)

My first publicity photo for CBS. I had such a ball
promoting the show.

(COURTESY OF CBS)

I thanked her.

Then there was a pause.

"Do you have a moment to talk?" she asked, her voice sounding slightly more informal.

"Sure," I said.

"May I ask you a question?"

"Okay."

"Who are you?" she asked. "And why are you doing this?"

I told her about myself and my other ideas. I explained that I was trying to start my career, but absent a job offer, I wanted to get respected professionals to write letters acknowledging that I was a creative and talented person so I could get a job after high school or college.

"What grade are you in?" she asked.

"I'm a junior," I told her, adding, "in high school."

"Go to college," she said. "Get an education."

"I plan to, but I'd like to build a portfolio."

"I see," she said. "As I told you, I think your card is clever. The problem is it doesn't fall into what we do. But thank you."

"Thank *you*," I said.

"Tony, let me ask you one more question. Is this address on the envelope your correct home address?"

"Yes," I said.

"I'm going to send you something," she said.

A week later, a letter addressed to Tony Zuiker arrived from Hallmark. Inside, I found a letter from this woman addressed "To Whom It May Concern," explaining that

Tony Zuiker was a polite, talented, ambitious young man with a gift for writing and thinking creatively. She described our acquaintance and encouraged whomever I showed this letter to to take me, and my talent, seriously.

I was blown away that this woman took the time to send such a letter. Hell, I was blown away she took me seriously—and thinking back on it, I still am. It was such a cool and crucial thing for her to do, and she never had any idea how important it was to me. I read the letter dozens of times before carefully placing it in a folder labeled "Portfolio." Then it went in my desk drawer—a prized possession.

27

Eddie, it turned out, saved newspapers. After he killed himself, I found among his possessions a *Las Vegas Sun* from 1982 with an article about the attempted murder of Frank Rosenthal ("Car Bomb Blasts Lefty") and a *Chicago Tribune* from June 19, 1986, reporting the death of mobster Anthony Spilotro ("Tony Spilotro's Fate Seems Dead Certain"). Spilotro and his brother Michael had driven to a hunting lodge in rural Indiana for a meeting with a mob boss and both ended up beaten and buried in a cornfield. "Tony Spilotro's vicious little life had more than run its course," the *Tribune* reported. "The remarkable thing is that such a truly evil little human being lived as long as he did."

"[Spilotro] was so powerful in Las Vegas that all he had to do was give the word and people who annoyed him were marked for a quick death," the paper noted. "But the other night, when Tony and his brother Michael went out of their car for the last time, they forgot one thing. They were in Chicago."

Through my mom, I learned that my dad had been in Chicago when the Spilotro hit went down, and though he had no connection to anyone involved, he took it as a sign to return to Vegas. Eddie had been looking for contacts in his old hometown, but for whatever reason, the doors there didn't open for him. One of his first stops when he got back to Vegas was the Tropicana, where my mom was now working.

After spotting her dealing blackjack, he stormed across the casino, eager for a confrontation. She was surprised when he arrived at her table. She didn't know he had come back to town. With one look, she knew he was drunk and so readied herself for trouble. He leaned in and asked, "What the hell is Tony up to, thinking about changing his name? And you—you're *allowing* this?"

Apparently, in a conversation they had had months earlier, my mom had mentioned that I had been thinking about changing my last name so that it sounded more Italian.

It was true, I had told her that—but I'd said it as a joke after watching a *Godfather* marathon. She probably told Eddie it was a joke, too. But seeing his Vegas disappear along with his own failures, and then hearing that his son wanted to ditch his last name, was more than Eddie could handle.

He was at the age when most men go through an identity crisis. Eddie was going through a catastrophe. I no longer had contact with him, no idea what he was doing with himself. Nor did I want to.

As a high school senior, I was ready to put those painful memories behind me. In January 1987, I was given a partial speech scholarship to the University of La Verne, a small private college outside Los Angeles. With the pressure of getting into school off, I relaxed for the rest of the year. Instead of studying like a madman, I channeled my energy into inventing sports-themed dice games. I loved sports, numbers, and being creative, and these little games obsessed me.

They fit in my pocket and I played them all the time. So did my friends. We'd go to a bar, order drinks, divide up into teams, set up the game, and roll the dice. They were fun. I thought I could sell them to Mattel and make a mint.

Dustin had stars in his eyes, too, and the two of us, full of the confidence of seniors who were coasting while dreaming of big futures, decided we needed new haircuts—and not just any haircuts. We wanted the freshest hip-hop styles on the street, and there was only one place to get them. It was a barbershop on D Street, located in the heart of Vegas's black neighborhood, and Scott Cheney, best known as Mr. C, owned and ran the place. He was to this corner of town what Wayne Newton was to the Strip—a superstar. Every notable black dude in the city got his hair cut there, including Lou Rawls, Billy Dee Williams, and the UNLV basketball star Spiderman Burns.

So imagine Dustin and I walking through the door: two white kids with shaggy hair. Actually, never mind the hair. We were two white kids crossing a sacred barrier, a barrier that may never have been crossed by a couple of Caucasian teenagers. But that was the point. All heads in the barbershop turned when we walked in, scared but with our chests puffed out, trying to come off as confident. Then Mr. C pierced us with his eyes, turning us into two pieces of undercooked shish kebab as he said hello and then took us ahead of his other customers.

The looks from the black guys we passed in line were deadly. Mr. C didn't care. That was his point. He was having fun at our expense. He must have figured that we could handle it if we had come to his shop. He knew his regulars would be pissed off, and they were. The comments and insults and threats flew back and forth. Mr. C loved every minute. This was his shop—and his show. I pretended not to hear anything and stared straight ahead, keeping my mouth shut until Mr. C put his hand atop my head, like a tight-fitting cap, and studied me in the mirror before getting to work.

"Could you please watch out for the mole under my right ear?" I asked in a voice that sounded shakier than intended.

With his hand still on top of my head, Mr. C immediately bent my neck to the side, searched for the sensitive area I had declared off-limits, and parked his razor right next to the mole.

"Shit, that's the first thing coming off," he said.

Eventually we relaxed some and appreciated the scene as much as we did our new haircuts, which were as tight as we'd hoped. Before we left, Mr. C pointed his razor at us and said, "Next time you come back bring me a Coke and a bag of Funions. If anyone gives you trouble, tell 'em you're going to Mr. C's." That had the opposite effect on

David. My stepdad put an end to Mr. C's. He didn't want me going into that part of town.

"I can save you the trouble of getting your ass kicked by doing it myself," he said.

It wasn't worth an argument. No matter what I said, David wasn't going to understand my reasons for going to Mr. C's. Of course, for me, it was part of growing up, and out. All of this happened around my graduation from Chaparral High. After anticipating the milestone for four years, the actual day was a bummer. Eddie didn't show up at the ceremony, and my mom pointed a camera in my face the whole time, explaining she wanted to remember this day that I wanted to forget. I was just ready to move out and go to college.

In September, my mom drove me to La Verne, crying as I unpacked, and we said goodbye. Aside from taking out a ten-thousand-dollar loan to supplement my scholarship, which put me in the hole before I started, I adapted to college immediately. I wasn't used to the excessive partying I found in the dorm, but I made friends easily and loved staying up talking late into the night. It seemed as if school might be a nonstop social event.

It wasn't. Classes were arduous, and my schedule grew more demanding once the forensics season began. There were only three of us on the team, but we were dedicated, as was our coach, Bob Rivera, who took me under his wing and became a trusted confidant. In his midsixties, Bob was extremely well read, passionate about speech, and an enthusiastic supporter of the SAE fraternity, which he got me to join. For me, the best part of competing was driving to the events. We sang fraternity songs and told stories.

At tournaments, I struggled to break against opponents more skilled and talented than those I had faced in high school. However, Dustin, now in his senior year in high school, benefited from my exposure to all this new material. After seeing Kevin Spengel and Chris Mancini from Bradley University take first place in Dramatic Duo at the National Forensic Association championships, I bought the play they performed, tailored it for Dustin, and told him to do it for Dramatic Interpretation. With college-level material, he was the Kobe Bryant of high school debate that year. I saw him walk out of one tournament with eight trophies.

After the speech scholarships were canceled at the end of the year, I spent my sophomore year at nearby Mount San Antonio College and then Cal Poly Pomona. I tried to stay close to my friends, but when Arizona State University offered a speech scholarship, I moved to Tempe. While I could handle the more challenging coursework, I floundered socially. The worst day was when I moved into the SAE house. My new roommate, a varsity swimmer, saw me put old Speed Racer sheets I'd brought from home on my bed, and that ended any chance I had at establishing credibility among my fraternity brothers.

Soon after, I moved into an apartment with a friend who was as studious as I was, but also just as broke. We were miserable—and hungry. One night I heated a can of

SpaghettiOs with a Bic lighter, and that was a treat. We stole sugar packets from Taco Bell and saved our Pizza Hut drink cups so we could sneak free refills. The lone bright spot came when I wrote a competitive piece exploring race, titled "They Call Me Anglo, but They Call You Sambo," about two white kids who get their hair cut in a black barbershop. My performance was good enough for third place in a national competition.

Later that summer, I reprised my performance in Mr. C's barbershop, in front of a full shop of customers, who gave me a standing ovation. I gave a copy of the piece and my trophy to Mr. C, who called me afterward to ask if I'd write a poem for his girlfriend. He wanted to get her back. So I did—and it worked.

But none of those feats was enough to keep me at ASU. Frustrated and starving there, I transferred to the University of Nevada, Las Vegas, and moved back home.

28

One night, after I had settled back into my old bedroom at home, my mom and David asked if I had any regrets about transferring to UNLV. They knew I had enjoyed my independence. But I nodded at the plate of food in front of me, a snack I'd prepared earlier. I loved not being hungry anymore.

"I'm good," I said. "Everything's cool."

I thrived at school. My ethnic studies professor, Dr. Roosevelt Fitzgerald, took a liking to me after he read my piece "They Call Me Anglo, but They Call You Sambo." He was an older man, slowed physically by several bypass surgeries, but still intellectually sharp. I interned for him. We had many challenging debates in and out of the classroom. He patted me on the back when I joined the Black Students Organization. He knew I was pushing the boundaries, but he let me figure them out for myself.

At the time, I was reading Black Arts Movement writers such as Sonia Sanchez, Maya Angelou, Nikki Giovanni, and Hoyt W. Fuller. At the Black Students Organization's annual talent contest, I performed Kimmika Williams's poem "It Ain't Easy to Be Different," which I found in an anthology.

As with joining the organization itself, I knew my performance was risky and might offend some people who didn't think I belonged, but my sense of commitment and passion was so strong that I looked past the obstacles in order to do what I felt was right, which was to share poetry that I thought was moving and meaningful. Indeed, my reading was met with a mixed reaction. "We still have a long way to go," the organization's president said as we shook hands afterward. "I guess that's why we're in school," I said. "We're learning."

Later that year I threw myself into fund-raising efforts for a couple students needing help. I helped produce a show that contributed eight thousand dollars toward medical expenses for my former high school speech teammate Christian Fisher, who'd lost his hand in a staging accident in a UNLV theater production. Then a girl in my public speaking class, Valerie Pida, revealed that she had been diagnosed with terminal cancer but had no medical insurance, and I raised thirteen thousand dollars for her by selling one of my dice games at UNLV basketball games.

I was honored as Student of the Week, and in a brief ceremony in the student union, the university's president put his hand on my shoulder and said, "I sincerely hope God's got a great place for you up in heaven." With graduation a month away, I simply hoped God could find me a job.

That fall, I enrolled in graduate courses in sociology

at UNLV, intending to get my PhD, and as part of that experience I signed up to teach Public Speaking 101. On the first day of class, I sat at one of the desks as if I were a student and eavesdropped on the conversations around me. A couple students asked if anyone knew about the professor. "He's new," someone said. I watched the clock tick past the hour when class was scheduled to start. A couple students grew antsy. "What's up with this dude, Tony Zuiker?" someone said. "The guy's late," another added. "Aren't the professors supposed to show up on time?"

Suddenly I stood up.

"Hello, everyone. I'm your professor, Tony Zuiker." I turned to the kid near me. "And actually, I arrived early—before anyone else."

The talking ceased instantly. Smiles turned to looks of fear, horror, and confusion. I walked to the front of the room and milked the moment until I was absolutely certain that I had connected with everyone in the room.

"Here's the first lesson I'm going to teach you about public speaking," I said. "Never underestimate your audience."

They hated me, of course—that day and every other. I also resented them for grousing every time I assigned a short paper or announced a quiz. By the end of the year, I realized I wasn't cut out for academics. I quit school and ended my flirtation with becoming Dr. Zuiker. I didn't know what to do next. I was interested in advertising, but I couldn't see a way to break into that business. With my gut telling me to do something creative, I considered my options and decided to turn my dice games into a business.

I raised a few thousand dollars from David's friends at the restaurant, including a captain named Bruno Petrini, who praised me for being a go-getter, and turned my bedroom into a game factory. I made dozens of games for every major sport—football, baseball, basketball, and hockey. The kits included a board, a pair of dice, score sheets, and a key card. Everything fit in a tiny plastic bag.

On the business license I bought for a few bucks, I named my enterprise Vend-A-Game International. Though I lacked experience, my instincts were on target. I bought two vending machines, filled them with games, and placed them in a popular arcade on Tropicana Avenue. I told the arcade's manager that I'd split my profits with him fifty-fifty. I checked them twice a week and usually found seventy or eighty bucks waiting for me.

After a couple of months, I thought I could sell the company for a lot of money, and I got the idea that I could attract top bidders if I could get some press for Vend-A-Game. I sent a letter about my company, along with two games, to Arlene Vigoda, a writer for the Life section of *USA Today*. In addition to describing the games, I added a short profile of the company's dynamic young founder, me, and then offered her an exclusive scoop: No one knew it yet, but the company was for sale for $10 million.

> I hate to sell the business after building it
> from the ground up. Each vending machine
> is special to me, as is every game. But as a
> businessman, I know it's the right time to sell.

> Sincerely,
> Tony Zuiker
> Founder and President
> Vend-A-Game International

> PS—If, after you print the story, you get any
> responses from interested parties, please ask
> them to contact me at the return address on
> the envelope.

I didn't see how she could *not* write a story. But I didn't hear back from Ms. Vigoda. After several months of dutifully checking each day's *USA Today*, I got the number for the paper's Washington, DC, office and asked to speak with her. A woman picked up after the first ring.

"Arlene Vigoda," she said.

"Hello, Ms. Vigoda," I said. "My name is Tony Zuiker. A few months ago, I sent you a couple of NFL board games. I also included the dice."

I paused.

"Yes?"

"I wanted you to run an article about my company in the Life section."

There was a moment of silence.

"Yes, I remember," she said. "I got your letter. I threw it away, along with your games."

Then, *click*. She hung up.

"She hung up on you?" my friend Rico said when I told him the story. "That's total disrespect."

"Who cares about that," I said. "She threw out two of my games!"

Soon I moved to Plan B.

I wrote a letter to Jill Barad, the then chairwoman and CEO of Mattel. She was the superstar of corporate America at the time. She had started as a $38,000-a-year product manager and risen to the company's number one position, earning a multimillion-dollar salary. She was powerful, envied, and influential. I wanted her to discover me.

I followed up my letter with a call to her office. Her assistant redirected me to a marketing/PR executive who listened to me pitch my business, my background, and my hope of getting a job there. He said there was a shareholders meeting coming up in El Segundo, California, and he'd take me out for a cup of coffee if I could make it there.

If I could make it there? *Nothing* was going to keep me from that shareholders meeting. To me, it was an opportunity.

"That would be great," I said. "I'll try to make it."

Less than a month later, I drove to El Segundo. I arrived two hours early and walked into the ballroom at the

Marriott hotel wearing a new Kmart suit I had bought for the occasion. It was actually a new bad habit I had developed: For any important event or meeting, I purchased a new outfit at Kmart. In the hotel's gift shop, I also bought a disposable camera and took pictures of the Mattel signs set up in the ballroom. When Jill Barad finally took the stage, I might as well have been staring at the Best Actress winner at the Academy Awards.

Hanging on every word she uttered about Mattel's future, I tried to picture where I might fit in at the company. I had overheard someone mention that a portion of the meeting offered shareholders the chance to ask the executives questions, and I was intending to introduce myself and pitch my board games, until the guy next to me, a stockbroker, overheard me practicing out loud. He asked what I was doing and then advised against it.

"Really?" I said.

"It's not the right forum for that," he explained. "You'll probably be escorted out of here."

Nearly three hours later the meeting broke up and I sought out the Mattel executive I had spoken to on the phone. We met in the hotel restaurant, and over coffee, he listened again to me talk about my games. He even looked through an album of photographs I'd taken of my friends playing them in my bedroom. I wanted him to be able to see them having fun.

"Do you understand how difficult it is to work here in the lab?" he asked.

"No," I said.

"You need to know," he told me. "You need to know how the whole business works. They have sections of this company where they hire people just to move Barbie's arm to see how high it will reach."

"I just want a job," I said. "I'll sweep floors. I'll do anything. I have a real knack for this thing. I think if you show Jill Barad my games—"

He pushed the photo album back across the table and said he wasn't going to show my games to Jill or anyone else. Then the meeting ended. I called him a few times over the summer, until he quit answering. As he said, my games were clever, but they weren't professional, not at the level of Mattel—and, as he made me realize, neither was I.

But if I wasn't that person I wanted to be, who was I? Just a kid with a couple of vending machines and a lot of ambition? That wasn't enough for me. I didn't have an answer yet, but I did possess one thing that helped offset the disappointment. It was my letter from the woman at Hallmark, and when I felt dejected or lost, I pulled that letter out of my desk drawer and reread it.

Tony Zuiker is a talented young man with a gift for writing and thinking creatively.

29

It wasn't supposed to be this hard. Where was the Reagan-era promise that every college graduate could get a good job with a decent salary? The best I could do following the failure of Vend-A-Game International was a job busing tables at Alias Smith & Jones, a local restaurant off the Strip. I knew it was temporary, but I resented every hour I spent there. I'd been in grad school. I had an education. I was a creative person. What was I doing wrong?

If you truly are creative, though, ideas will continue to surface no matter what you are doing. Then the challenge is to not get too frustrated or lose hope while you figure out ways to make those ideas pay off. Still, I had doubts that I would ever find the secret. After all, some people didn't—like Eddie.

Although I rarely thought about my dad, I was mindful of his failure. On top one day; struggling to hang on the next. Part of my drive could be attributed to my determination not to end up like him. It was a subject that didn't need to be discussed. Indeed, Eddie had been back in Vegas for months before my mom mentioned it to me. He was repairing slot machines, she said.

I burned inside from the knowledge that I wasn't doing much better than my dad. After work one day, I bought the latest edition of *Communication Arts*, a thick advertising journal I had remembered reading in an advertising class at school. It was full of photos of the best billboards and print ads from around the world, and I was craving that sort of inspiration. I took it home and looked at every page at least three times. I felt like I could do that kind of work—so why wasn't I?

A few days later, after pulling an all-night shift, I left Alias Smith & Jones and took a walk along Tropicana Avenue. It was morning, and the sun felt good after ten hours in a dark, air-conditioned restaurant. A sign in front of a sex shop caught my eye and I stopped. In red letters against a yellow backdrop, it said, "The BIGGEST Sex Store in America." I chuckled at the innuendo—then, a moment later, thought, Hey, what if I can make a sign that's even better?

I checked my watch. It was a little after six in the morning, too early to go into a porn shop without feeling weird and pathetic, but I told myself it was "research." After a quick browse, I went home, sat in front of my PC, loaded my paintbrush tools, and mocked up a picture of three blow-up dolls from the chest up with a caption that read "Picking Up Air Heads Just Got Easier."

After incorporating the store's logo and a small subhead—"America's Largest Sex Store"—I went to Kinko's and printed a version that was about the size of a long carton of cigarettes. I was delighted when I saw the finished copies roll out of the machine. The girl behind the counter laughed as she rang me up.

"Really?" she asked as she handed them back to me. "Are you serious?"

"What do you think?" I asked.

"Funny," she said.

Encouraged by her reaction, I put the prototype into a grocery bag and went back to the sex store. I walked up to the counter and rang the penis-shaped bell. The same woman I'd noticed behind the counter earlier that morning stuck her head through a door: "What's up?"

"I want to talk to the manager," I said.

"He's in the back," she said. "Why do you want him?"

"You know that sign in the window of your store?" I said. "I have a new one for him—a new concept I want him to look at."

A moment later, a heavyset man stepped out, holding a can of Diet Coke. He had on a white shirt, black Dockers, and suspenders. He sized me up with small, dark, joyless eyes and began giving me attitude before I said a word. He thought I was there to return a toy or video and ask for a refund. I assured him that I wasn't there to be a pain in the ass. I had come to offer help.

"What do you want to do for me?" he asked.

"Sir, I have this billboard," I said, gathering nerve. "I saw your billboard out there advertising your shop. I didn't think it's creative, and I made a new one up for you that I think would be cool."

"Where is it?" he asked.

I pulled my work out of the grocery bag and put it on the counter.

"It's an awesome piece of artwork," I said.

He flipped it around, studied it for a minute, and nodded.

"I like it," he said. "It's funny. What do you want for it?"

"I don't know," I said. "Make me an offer."

He stared the other way, doing some kind of math. He muttered something about forty thousand people, being open twenty-four hours a day, and a few other things, none of which I understood.

"I'll give you five hundred cash or a thousand in store credit," he said.

"I'll take the cash," I said.

He opened the register and peeled off five crisp one-hundred-dollar bills. I folded them in half and jammed them deep into my pocket. Outside, I got in my car, and let out a loud, celebratory whoop. I'd sold a project that had been mine from start to finish—A Tony Zuiker Production.

I was on my way.

30

After my success at the sex shop, I quit Alias Smith & Jones to make more billboards. As I told my friends, I was in advertising now. I handed out tons of fliers to local businesses, and despite a few follow-up meetings, I didn't make any more sales. Discouraged, I stayed afloat by betting on sports, but that was about as lucrative as busing tables. It wasn't a career. I had nothing to latch on to. I felt like a loser.

One day I shared my frustrations with Dustin, who was in Los Angeles, trying to make it as an actor and writer. He seemed to be doing well—better than me, anyway. He had landed a few small jobs, gotten callbacks on auditions, and sounded hopeful about his future. He told me that he was using monologues I'd written for him in high school for his auditions, and added, "Tony, people really respond to your stuff. You should write more."

But I wasn't a writer. I wasn't doing anything. Which must have worried Dustin. Soon after we spoke, his father called and told me to come to his office to talk about a job.

Right away, I knew I had done something to irk Gary. It turned out he was upset with me for not dressing up.

"Tony, this is a job interview with the city's top brokerage," he said sternly. "You don't wear a sweatshirt."

I understood, and apologized. Gary was warm, principled, and tough—but in this case it was tough love. He was someone who looked impeccable whenever he went out, and he wanted me to know those kinds of details mattered when trying to make an impression. He lectured me about striving for perfection because, as he said, "It's that kind of attention to detail that will make you successful one day."

Those talks weren't always easy to take, but now I appreciate every word. He gave me the thick skin I would need in Hollywood.

Despite my wardrobe, I ended up as the firm's new wire operator. Back then, brokers wrote up transaction tickets—buy, sell, option—on pieces of paper and put their orders in a pneumatic cylinder, which sped through a network of tubes to my desk in the wire room. Mine was a glass-walled nerve center for all transactions. As the trades came in, I read the tickets and sent the transaction information to New York via teletype.

Despite the volume of trades, there was no room for mistakes, not the slightest error. A mistake, as Gary and others reminded me dozens of times during my training, could cost thousands of dollars or more, depending on the trade size.

I understood.

But there was nothing like learning that lesson firsthand, as I did on day one. Just two hours into my training, Gary flew into the office and barked, "Get off! Get off the damn wire!" He wasn't rude; he was on point, and doing his job, as he should have been. The Immune Response Corporation, a large pharmaceutical company that had soared to record highs on the promise of a new HIV drug, was in free fall after news broke that the medication had failed testing. Investors were bailing, and Gary didn't want a trainee on the desk at such a crucial time.

Nor did I want to be there. I couldn't have handled the volume of trades or the pressure of having Gary and other brokers breathing down my neck.

The job didn't get any easier. On October 23, 1993, Steve Wynn demolished the Dunes Hotel, one of the original old hotels on the Strip. More than two hundred thousand people turned out to watch the building get blown up. In its place, the billionaire mogul announced plans to build the Bellagio, a hotel that would be the most luxurious in Vegas. The spectacle generated heavy trading of his company's stock, as well as other Vegas hotel stocks.

Traffic in the wire room was the busiest I'd seen in three months on the job. However, now that I was more experienced, I was left to handle the trades on my own. I soon wished someone else had been in the hot seat. While entering a buy order for five thousand shares of Circus Circus (ticker symbol: CIR), I inadvertently entered the symbol for the Mirage (MIR). It was about a ten-thousand-dollar mistake.

I'd never felt time move as slowly as it did while I sat at my desk waiting for Gary to tell me he wanted to see me in his office. It felt like five hours; it was more like forty-five minutes before my phone rang. When I walked

in, Gary and several of the firm's top traders were waiting for me, smoking cigarettes. The clouds of gray smoke
conjured up images of Dante's Hell.

"Anthony, sit down," Gary said.

I saw one empty chair a few steps away. I prayed my
knees wouldn't give out before they got me there.

"Yes, sir," I said.

"Anthony—"

"Yes, sir. I'm sorry—"

He held up his hand. He didn't want me to talk.

"I know you're sorry," he continued. "But—"

"I am sorry," I interrupted.

"How do you spell Charlie?" he asked in a calm voice,
an eerily calm voice.

"C—"

"Stop," he said. "How do you spell Margaret?"

"M—"

"Stop!" he said. "How the hell do you confuse CIR
with MIR?"

"I don't—"

"Stop," he said. "I don't know either."

"I know. I'm very—"

"Sorry doesn't fix it," he said. "You're a bright kid. I
know you're conscientious. I know you feel terrible."

"Are you going to fire me?"

"No," he said. "What kind of lesson would that teach
you?"

Days later, Gary made a point of letting me know that
he didn't hold a grudge and wanted to put me on track

to become a broker. It would be a year or two down the road, he said, but I was sharp and had the tools to do well in the business.

He gave me a supportive pat on the back.

But deep down I knew I couldn't last another year or two on the wire desk. I was too impatient. I didn't want to wait that long before I started making some dough.

31

My friend Rico was rolling in it. Now a bellman at the MGM Grand, he called one day literally panting with excitement.

"Man, I just got a two-grand tip," he said.

"What the—"

"Two thousand dollars!" he said.

"Who gave you that much money?" I asked.

"It was DeBartolo," he said. "The dude from San Francisco."

He was talking about Edward DeBartolo Jr., the owner of the San Francisco 49ers. DeBartolo had made a fortune owning shopping malls and used it to win NFL championships. Rico had been a wide receiver in high school. His dream was to play for the 49ers. Seeing De-Bartolo gave him an idea.

"Tony, he just checked in," he said. "He's here for four days. This is my chance to get on the field. How the hell can I do it?"

I offered to write him a letter. With all the writing I'd done for speech competitions and people like my old barber, Mr. C, I knew I had a knack for persuasion. Rico agreed, and told me to go for it. I researched DeBarto-lo's career and wrote a page-and-a-half letter from Rico, asking for a tryout with the team. I told Rico to hand it to DeBartolo when he checked out.

"Should I say anything about it?" he asked. "Should I try to explain?"

"No, just give him the letter," I said.

A couple of months later, DeBartolo's office contacted Rico and invited him to training camp. After we were done high-fiving each other, Rico bought a machine that threw him passes and worked out until rookie camp started. He reminded me of Rocky Balboa training for his fight against Apollo Creed. He knew the odds were against him. But part of living the dream is trying to make it come true.

After a week at camp, he flew back home. He'd been dismissed in the first round of cuts. He wasn't upset in the least. He'd had the best time of his life, and he brought back an actual pro jersey with his name on it, 49er work-out gear, and memories that would last forever.

I envied such disappointments. But my chance arrived soon enough. In late 1993, I accepted a position in the broker's training program at Merrill Lynch. The job included delivering mail, but I would be trained as a broker and have my own desk—and I'd be off the wire desk. The hard part was telling Gary. He didn't say much. I knew he wasn't happy. At the end of my last day there, I went into his office and thanked him one more time. He wished me luck.

I needed it. On my first day at Merrill Lynch, I failed the mandatory pretest for prospective brokers. I should have been let go on the spot. But the branch's star financial consultant, as they called their brokers, Janie Thomas, put in a word with Merrill's branch manager, David Glover, and suddenly my failed test score didn't matter anymore.

I was sent to the mailroom, where I assisted the financial consultants and studied for the broker's exam. I put tremendous pressure on myself to pass even if only to show Gary that I'd made the right choice. But I had my doubts. The job itself was more pressure than the wire desk. On April 22, 1994, the day former president Richard Nixon died, months of pressure finally got to me. A large, red, and painful knot appeared on the side of my head. As the day progressed, the redness spread down my neck. It also itched.

I sat up all night worrying that I had cancer. In the morning, I saw a doctor and his questions exacerbated my concerns.

"Tell me about your sexual activity," he said.

"What?" I said, wondering what that had to do with anything I'd come in to have checked.

"Are you sleeping with anyone? Are you active?"

"Nothing to boast about," I said.

"Do you use protection?"

"Yes," I said. "Why?"

"This rash on your head looks like an immune problem," he said. "I'm not saying it's HIV or anything related."

"HIV?" I asked.

"I'd like you to get tested."

For two days, I thought I was going to die from AIDS.

Logic told me that I fell into the zero-risk category, but I still worried until the test results came back negative. The official diagnosis ended up herpes zoster—or shingles, a painful virus-based rash often associated with stress. I endured several weeks of discomfort as the red blisters spread across my scalp, face, and neck. I reassured my coworkers it wasn't contagious.

It all led up to the Series 7 broker's exam. Passing the six-hour test, administered by the Financial Industry Regulatory Authority, was a necessary step if you wanted to trade for a firm. My test was being given in San Diego, and I drove there early in the morning wearing a suit I'd borrowed from David, hoping that a sharp look would help my confidence. After the grueling exam, I felt great about my answers. To celebrate, I drove straight to the beach, ran across the sand, and dove in the water.

A few weeks later, my results came. I'd scored a 92—I passed. As far as I was concerned, I was set. I was going to be a millionaire.

In reality, I was assigned to make cold calls in an effort to bring in new business. I was too insecure to be effective at asking strangers to come in and entrust me with their money. I barely had any of my own. So for eight hours a day, I said, "Hi, this is Tony Zuiker from Merrill Lynch," and then I heard the click of a hang-up. Sometimes I heard worse. The rejection was demoralizing. It wasn't fun going into work.

By this time, I had moved into an apartment of my own on Tropicana and Koval. It turned out to be the same complex as David's friend Bruno, who had helped back Vend-A-Game International. He had been fond of saying, "Tony, if you weren't so smart, you'd be rich." After hearing I was at Merrill Lynch, he came in one day with twenty-five thousand dollars and told me to invest it. Several of his friends asked for the same treatment. Even a priest from Italy sent money.

"Pick some dogs and put them to work," Bruno said.

Pretty soon I was making investments for all these people and churning out some pretty decent commissions. But the guy I worked under took nearly all of it. He said he was entitled to it for training me.

My sense of injustice could have easily derailed my career before it took off, but that was done for me. In September 1994, Janie Thomas was suddenly fired. In what the *New York Times* called a "bizarre episode," Janie was accused of "creating phony and inflated accounts for her clients." Her "fabrications" totaled about twenty million dollars, and her list of clients included singer Paul Anka. Strangely, she didn't appear to have stolen any money or done anything that would have affected her compensation.

"As best we can tell, she seems to have wanted to create a mystique about herself that would lead to client referrals and other new business," a Merrill spokesman told the *Times*.

As soon as the scandal broke, Janie and her husband, Bobbie, who also worked on the desk, disappeared. Their car was found at Los Angeles International Airport. Rumors circulated that they had fled the country.

In 2004, Bobbie Thomas would turn himself in after a decade of hiding while Janie's whereabouts remained a mystery. The company would also voluntarily repay some seventeen million dollars to clients.

In the meantime, though, a team from the Securities and Exchange Commission descended on our branch and combed through every computer and document in the office. Merrill also sent a new regime from New York to run the operation while the company figured out the damages. I didn't know who anyone was. One morning I walked into work carrying a couple of heavy FedEx boxes. I set them down on my desk and then noticed a man in a dark blue suit next to me.

"Hey, good morning, champ," I said.

Startled by the boxes landing on the desk, the guy bolted up from his chair and snapped, "Did you just call me 'champ'?"

I nodded.

"I am the vice president of this entire company, of all of Merrill Lynch," he said. "Do you understand?"

"Yes, sir," I said.

"Do you understand what that means?" he asked.

"Yes, sir."

"I don't think you do," he said.

"Excuse me?" I said.

"No, I won't excuse you," he said. "You're fired."

"What?"

"Get your shit and get out of here. Right now."

"Are you serious?"

"Yeah. I am. Take a walk."

Everyone in the firm stared as I grabbed my belongings and left the office. Shell-shocked, I sat in my car, wondering why I had wasted all that time studying for my broker's license only to be fired by some asshole having a bad day because of Janie and Bobbie Thomas.

What about my job? What about my commissions? What about my rent? What about my future?

In the big picture, it was a lucky break. But at that moment I was dead in the water.

32

From my experience at the brokerages, I knew I wasn't going to become another Gary Abraham. I had to be myself. I still thought that meant being creative, and in search of some guidance, I sent a sample of my ideas to a former advertising professor of mine at UNLV. He had his own company on the side and I thought he might have an entry-level position.

He called as soon as he received my package, which I thought might be a positive sign. It wasn't. He said my work was talentless and the last thing I should consider was a career in advertising. He also chewed me out for wasting his time, adding, "I hope this helped."

As always, I vowed to show him how wrong he was. I set my sights on getting into the advertising and marketing department at the Mirage. It was the best hotel in Vegas, the centerpiece of Steve Wynn's operation, and I figured they had to be on the lookout for bright new talent. I mocked up several magazine ads and sent them on spec to John Schadler, the vice president of advertising. A few days later, his secretary called and set up a meeting.

"See," I told Rico. "They recognized genius."

"Are you sure they had the right number?" he joked.

It turned out to be a joke—a cruel one. When I entered John's office, he was at his desk, watching the stock ticker scroll across a TV on the opposite side of the room. He let me sit there for a minute or two before turning away from the TV and directing his attention to me. But he looked confused.

"Who do you think you are, sending me ideas and asking for a job?" he said.

"What?" I asked.

"I get submissions from everybody and their grand-mother," he continued. "They come in every day of the week."

"I thought my ideas were good," I said.

"This is a billion-dollar business," he said. "We don't use submissions from people off the street."

"I'm just trying to get a job."

"Take the appropriate steps," he said. "Fill out an application with HR. Check back in six months. Work your way up."

I didn't get it. Why did these busy people take time out of their days just to chastise me simply for trying to get ahead? At least this meeting had provided some useful information. *Go to HR. Fill out an application.* Before I left the corporate offices, I found Human Resources and asked if there were any openings at the hotel. There was one for a tram driver. I thought, What the hell, and filled out an application. Months later, I went back in for an interview and left as the new tram driver.

I was assigned to the graveyard shift, from 7 p.m. to 4 a.m., and issued a uniform: a Hawaiian-print beach shirt, khaki pants, and brand-new white tennis shoes. On my first day, my boss, Chuck Nino, introduced me to my supervisor, a petite African-American lady named Tamika. As she explained, there wasn't much to the job other than fighting boredom. The tram went back and forth between the Mirage and Treasure Island and the driver told the passengers to watch their step as they got on and off, and answered their questions—though 90 percent of the time it was the same question: What time did the Mirage's volcano go off?

After a few months on the graveyard shift, I realized why Tamika had looked so bored. The job was the same every night. The shift started with the show crowds and the tourists; then came the partiers, loud and boisterous, carrying drinks and whooping it up between hotels; and then it was dead. Between 1:30 and 4 a.m., it was just me and the tram.

My challenge then was to battle the boredom. One night, I asked a Japanese lady to teach me a few phrases in Japanese. I started with five basic phrases that I used every shift: "Welcome to the Mirage," "My name is Anthony," "Every four minutes," "Watch your step," and "Goodbye." I wrote each one down phonetically in a little black book I carried in my pocket, practiced them, and then delighted a couple of Japanese tourists by answering their question in their own language.

That led me to collect those same phrases from every person I encountered speaking a foreign language. I wrote them down in Spanish, Chinese, Korean, French, Farsi,

Portuguese, Swedish, Russian, and more. After accumulating phrases in two dozen languages, I formalized the presentation in a new book, with a page for each country and a sticker of that country's flag. I titled it *The International Phonetic Language Book*, and on the first page I wrote, "There's no better way to respect the customers than to speak their language."

I used the book every night—it became my thing. People enjoyed being responded to in their own language, and it kept me amused.

Occasionally, there were some gaffes. One night a couple of Filipino kids came on board. I asked them how to say all the key phrases, and they helped out and left the tram waving an enthusiastic goodbye. A week later, a Filipino football team got on the tram and I gave them my talk. Instead of the usual friendly reaction, they backed away from me.

I had no idea what I had said. A Filipino woman with the group came up to me and explained my mistake.

"You said, 'Hello, do you have a girlfriend? I am gay.'"

Despite the occasional faux pas, my *International Phonetic Language Book* was a hit. Word of the book spread throughout the Mirage; other departments asked for copies, including security, the bell desk, and hospitality. Each department requested additional phrases specific to their jobs.

The effort impressed my boss, who took a few minutes to find out a little bit about me. When he heard that my background included speech and creative writing, he had me write some speeches for him. I said yes to every-thing, hoping word of my cleverness would spread all the way to Steve Wynn's office and result in a promotion, and a raise.

One night, a well-dressed woman got on the tram and noticed me using my booklet to engage the hotel guests. After waiting for me to finish talking to a couple, she asked if she could look through my book. After looking through several pages, she asked my name and dropped the book in her purse.

"Wait, ma'am," I said. "That's my only copy."

"That's fine," she said. "My name is Zelma Wynn. I'm Steve Wynn's mother. And I want to tell him about you."

I wasn't happy about giving her my best copy—I still had the original—but my name and phone number were printed in bold letters on the front page. I figured if I wasn't going to give a copy directly to Steve Wynn, his mother was the next best thing. As it turned out, I never heard from Mr. Wynn, but that was all right. Other op-portunities came up as a result of my initiative.

33

After helping my boss, Chuck, with several speeches, I was rewarded with a promotion to baggage handler one day a week. The job was more physically demanding than I had imagined. But it was a necessary step to a better-paying bellman job, which I wanted, and so I ignored the back pain from lifting and the barbs from the veteran handlers who thought I'd kissed butt to get my foot in their door.

A promotion arrived a few months later after I told Chuck either to put me on Sundays as a bellman or let me go back to the tram. I was getting slammed doing both and not making any money. Plus, my promotion continued to anger the other bellmen.

"Better watch your back," one guy warned in the elevator. "I'm going to kick your ass after work."

It didn't happen, but it might have been worth it for what I made in tips. On my one Sunday of checking people in and out, I averaged between $200 and $250 in tips—half of what I made every two weeks driving the tram. After a few more months, I was bumped up to a full-time bellman. The other baggage handlers were also promoted, eliminating a bad situation.

Being a bellman, I needed a new skill set, a sixth sense for anticipating the needs of guests. I dealt with every type of person, race, ethnicity, and income level, including honeymooners, foreign dignitaries, and celebrities—Nicolas Cage, Quentin Tarantino, Michael Jordan, and Tom Selleck, among others. All were good tippers.

Money was always the main topic of conversation among us. One time word went around that a major movie star was in the casino, playing multiple hands of blackjack for twenty-five grand a pop. We took turns running into the casino to see the stacks of chips. It was a cheap thrill.

A few weeks into my new job, I got a call for a *last*, meaning I was the last bellman in line to help anyone checking in and therefore the first one available to run the trivial errands that people call down for from their rooms. The call came from the dispatcher, a heavyset guy, six foot two, with droopy eyes. He talked and moved in slow motion and looked as if he was about to fall asleep.

"Yo, what do they need?" I asked.

"I don't know," he said. "It's room 605. See what the guy wants."

"Really?"

"Man, I'd do it," he said. "But I'm reading the sports page."

"No problem," I said.

"You keep the tip," he said. "They'll probably stiff you anyway."

I knew what he meant. The first time he had called me for a last, the guest asked me to get some mousse, hairspray, and gum. In that situation, the bellman goes downstairs to the gift shop, pays for the items out of his own pocket, and gets reimbursed by the guest. In my case, the guest never answered the door and I was out twenty-five bucks.

But that was the job. You never knew if you'd get stiffed or score a great tip. So I hustled up to room 605 and knocked on the door. When no one answered, I knocked again and said, "Bellman!" A half second later the door opened with a sudden swoosh that nearly sucked me inside. In front of me stood an enormous Persian man wearing only silk shorts. He was a mess. His hair was sticking straight up. His back was bleeding from scratch marks. He was also three miles high and grinning as though he was having the time of his life.

"Wolf! Good to see you, Wolf," he said.

Something about this guy was off. I took a step backward in order to get a better look. You never knew with guests. This guy clearly had been partying hard for a while. He was amped—and extremely glad to see me. I followed him inside his room, and he closed the door.

"Come in, Wolf," he said. "It's a crazy day, isn't it, Wolf?"

"I guess," I said.

"Good, Wolf."

Why was he calling me Wolf, I wondered. My name tag was clearly visible above my left breast pocket. It said, "Anthony, Chicago."

"Wolf, how are you doing?" he asked.

"I'm okay," I said.

He put a hand on my shoulder.

"You know why I call you Wolf?" he said.

"No, why?"

"Because of that Tarantino movie, *Pulp Fiction*," he said. "He calls the guy Wolf—the guy who handles everything for you."

Ah, I got it. The Harvey Keitel part.

"You're like my Wolf," he continued.

"Okay," I said again, hoping there was a tip in it for me.

"Just a minute, Wolf," he said.

He disappeared into his room and rummaged through his suitcase. I looked over his shoulder and saw maybe ten or twelve naked women, all in suggestive poses and gazing at themselves in the floor-to-ceiling mirrors along the wall. They were all as spaced out as the Persian guy, who stepped back into the entry.

"Wolf, help me out," he said. "Let's talk business."

He was holding a fistful of cash and shifting back and forth, as wired as I had ever seen anyone.

"Sir, what can I do for you?" I asked. "Do you want me to get you a girl?"

"Yes, yes, Wolf, that's exactly what I want," he said. "I need action. Wolf, I want action."

"With all due respect, sir," I said, nervously, "you have a number of beautiful women naked in your room right now."

"No, Wolf," he said, gesturing wildly with his hands. "I want fresh. Fresh girl. Fresh! Take care of me?" He put three hundred dollars in my hand. "For you, Wolf. Take care of me. Please."

"Thank you, sir," I said, trying not to stare at the money. But I was so happy I almost cried in front of him. "I'll do what I can."

I shut the door, walked down the hallway, and got in the guest elevator, which was against the rules. Bellmen were supposed to take the service elevator that went to the dispatch station. But I wasn't thinking clearly anymore. I was dazed from the money.

Downstairs, I realized I had no idea how to get him a girl, but the three crisp hundred-dollar bills he'd put in my hand motivated me to figure out something. I walked through the main lobby, past the buffet and the shops. I went to a phone booth and looked up escort services in the Yellow Pages. I ripped out an ad for the first place that caught my eye, Bunny Love. I copied the number onto a Mirage note card and returned to room 605.

I had been gone about ten minutes when the Persian guy opened the door with the same overzealous energy as before.

"Wolf!" he practically screamed. "How you doing, Wolf?"

I gave him the card.

"Here," I said. "Bunny Love. She's amazing. Call and she'll take care of you."

"Wolf, thank you very much," he said.

He counted out five more hundred-dollar bills and gave them to me. Now I had eight hundred in my pocket. About an hour and a half later, following lunch, the dispatcher told me to go back to 605 again. With a roll of his eyes, he said the guy was asking for me.

"It sounds like he's upset," the dispatcher said.

I had no idea what I might have done wrong. But I knew that calling one of those ads in the Yellow Pages was risky. Who knew what would show up at his door. He could have been ripped off, mugged, stabbed—God only knew what. I imagined twenty different scenarios, each one bad.

"Okay," I said. "I'll go right up."

After knocking on his door, I heard a commotion inside. Suddenly the door flew open and there was Mr. 605, now shirtless and in white pajama pants. He was a mess. But his bloodshot eyes widened as soon as he recognized me.

"Wolf, oh my God!" he said. "Hold on."

He took a gob of cash out of his pocket, pressed twelve hundred-dollar bills in my hand, and kissed me on the forehead.

"Wolf, she was magnificent."

Then he slammed the door.

Now I had two grand in my pocket. I'd never had that much money at once in my life. I thought I might have a nervous breakdown. Downstairs, back at the dispatch station, I played it cool. The dispatcher looked up and asked if I had taken care of the guest in 605. I said yes, it hadn't been a big deal.

"What'd you get?"

"Same garbage," I said. "Two bucks."

"I told you."

34

You never knew what could happen at the Mirage. One day a sultan from a Middle Eastern country checked in. He arrived with his family and entourage amid a fleet of limousines. A handful of children exited the car, all appearing to be between eight and twelve years old. As I got their luggage, a couple of the kids pranced around me holding little blue velvet bags filled with precious gems—diamonds, rubies, and sapphires.

"Look what I have," one said. "You like?"

Did I like? I hoped they would drop a couple in the grass so I could retire.

Altogether, their party totaled more than twenty people. I loaded up three brass carts with luggage. In the last limo, I actually found a live goat. He was scared, shriveled up, and dirty. I pulled him out with a rope and yanked him away from the flowers, which he tried to eat, before walking him up to the room.

After I had spent nearly an hour bringing up the carts, delivering the luggage to various rooms, and handing off the goat, the sultan stiffed me. I was still smarting when I got the call two days later to help check them out, but I did my job without complaint. I brought several carts to their room and knocked on the door. No one answered.

After a few minutes I swiped my access key and opened the door. A strong odor hit me.

With my hand over my mouth, I walked in and looked around. The enormous suite was empty, the Middle Eastern guests long gone, and the place was thoroughly trashed. The curtains were ripped and the bedsheets missing. I noticed a makeshift fire pit near the sliding glass doors leading out to the balcony, and there was blood splattered across the walls, floor, and furniture.

I didn't know where to look in order to figure out what had happened. Nor was I sure I wanted to know. Then something in the large potted plant near the corner caught my eye. I took a few steps forward, then stopped and put my hand over my mouth. Two hoofs were sticking up from the dirt. It was the goat—or what was left of it.

I had heard all kinds of stories about people doing freaky things in their rooms, including one Middle Eastern royal who insisted on having a gold toilet installed in his suite. But an animal sacrifice was a new addition to the list. Chuck hadn't heard of anything like it, either.

"Are you shitting me?" he asked.

"I saw the hooves sticking up out of the potted plant in the corner," I said. "And blood everywhere."

He scratched his head.

"Okay, go back to work and keep your mouth shut while I look into it."

An hour later, he walked up to me and turned his face to the side so no one could eavesdrop.

"Here's the deal," he said. "Don't mention a word about the room or anything you saw."

"Not a problem."

"It never happened, right?"

"I don't even know what you're talking about," I said.

Another time I was first in line on a busy day when I heard the dispatcher say, "Check-in. Villas." I allowed myself a very subtle fist pump. The villas were for high rollers and rich people, and they usually meant generous tips. I checked the reservation list and saw the name "R. Dangerfield." Even better, I thought, a celebrity. But you never knew with those guys. They could stiff you as easily as they could give you a grand, but generally the tips were generous.

I was at the curb with my cart when Rodney's limousine pulled up. When he got out, his eyes were bloodshot and he was in a great mood. I assumed he was baked.

"How you doing there, boy," he said, slapping me on the butt.

As I unloaded his luggage, he cracked jokes and made conversation with me and everyone else nearby. But when I stepped into his villa, I saw the place was a mess. Apparently housekeeping had missed it after the previous guests left. Wine bottles were on the floor, the bedsheets were strewn across the room, and plates of half-eaten food were on the bed and floor. The room stunk.

I didn't want Rodney to go in, but he pushed past me,

surveyed the damage, and then turned and faced me. He was livid.

"This piece-of-crap hotel," he yelled. "Dammit, I told them to make it all right. I've got to perform tonight. What's going on here?"

"I'm sorry, Mr. Dangerfield," I said. "I don't know what happened here."

"Goddamn it, kid," he said. "Get on the phone with housekeeping. Make them fix it. No, get me a new room."

"Yes, sir," I said.

While I called my boss, Rodney undid his suitcase and pulled out a leather satchel and a boom box. He took both into the bathroom and slammed the door. I could barely hear housekeeping on the phone, promising to make up the room immediately. It was Rodney's boom box. He was blasting Twisted Sister's classic "We're Not Gonna Take It" inside the marble bathroom and it was shaking the entire villa. After about ten minutes, the door flew open and Rodney banged out of there with the music still at full volume, as if the band were playing him off the stage.

"I want a new room, kid," he said. "And I want everything in this room to be exactly as I have it but in my new room. Got it?"

"Yes, sir," I said.

"Good," he said, before walking out the door.

I didn't move for about a minute. I went into the bathroom, and my eyes bugged out in disbelief. The bathroom counter was like an illegal pharmacy. He had laid out two vials of coke, with two long lines perfectly cut and drawn, four joints, two bottles of pills, and a razor blade. The music was blasting. I had no idea what to do. Should I call security? Should I flush the drugs down the toilet? Should I show them to housekeeping?

I thought, Screw it. I opened up his satchel, put the pills back in, stuck the joints in my jacket pocket, used the razor blade to put every speck of coke back in the vials, and packed it all back in the satchel. Then I turned off the boom box, unplugged it, and packed both back in his suitcase. When housekeeping showed up, his bags were stacked on my cart. I was waiting in front.

"Where's the next room?" I asked.

They led me to the neighboring villa, 17B, and left me to deal with the angry celebrity. I wheeled Rodney's luggage in and took out his satchel and boom box. I put them in the bathroom, plugged in the boom box, pressed rewind, and dumped out six pills, took out the two vials of coke, cut two of the longest and most perfect lines ever, and set the four joints on the counter as they had been in the previous room. I hit play on the boom box. Twisted Sister reverberated through that marble-filled room just as Rodney returned.

"Mr. Dangerfield," I said, turning around and playing up the service. "What else can I do for you?"

He laughed.

"You are the man," he said, giving me an enthusiastic whack across my back. "This hotel is fantastic. Hold on a minute, kid."

He fished out five hundred dollars from his pocket and pushed it into my hand.

"Thank you, sir," I said.

"You're thanking me?" he said with a laugh. "You did a helluva job, kid. You're going places. I can feel it."

PART VI

ROLLING THE
DICE

35

I didn't know where to put Eddie. Moving tentatively through my Sheraton Universal suite, I put him in the bedroom, the living room, the bathroom, and finally on the dining room table, thinking he might make a good centerpiece. I also tried his heavy marble urn as a door-stop. None of the places worked. Still holding the urn in my arms, I looked at the window. Eddie would have loved the view of the Hollywood Hills, but there wasn't a ledge. I needed a place to put my dad. If nothing else, my arms were tired.

"Damn, Eddie, you still aren't easy," I said.

I shouldn't have expected anything else. After twenty-five years of little to no contact, Eddie was back in my life and it required adjustments. For several days, I kept trying him in different spots. I didn't want him right in the middle of my life. Nor did I want to forget about him in a closet. He was on the coffee table when my assistant, Orlin, brought some scripts and mail from the office. As the two of us ate sushi, Orlin noticed the urn.

"Anthony, that is nice," he said. "Where'd you get it?"

"Vegas," I said.

"The mall?" he asked.

"No, the mortuary," I said. "My dad's ashes are in there."

"Oh my God," he said, suddenly leaning away.

Later, after we had spent a few hours working, Orlin tapped the urn with his pen and looked at me.

"I thought you didn't speak to your father," he said.

"No, not for most of my life."

"And now he's here?"

"I don't know," I said, shrugging my shoulders. "I want to do the right thing for him—whatever that means."

Eventually that meant putting Eddie next to an egg-shaped wish pot I had on a small shelf between the bar and the entry door. It looked as if I had a collection of some sort. I got in the habit of tapping the urn every time I came in or went out. Sometimes I said "Hello" or "Goodbye"; other times it was "See you later" or "How you doing?" It was very casual, very weird, and very ironic. After being out of touch for most of my life, I touched him, literally, every day. It was my way of finally coming to terms with him.

How long would that take?

It was impossible to say. But I knew that I'd have a sense when it was time to move Eddie to his final resting place, wherever that was.

My whole career was based on making moves that, during my days as a bellman, required educated guesswork. Back at the Mirage, I was making sixty thousand a year as a bellman. Although it was a decent salary, I knew that the unpredictability of working for tips, as well as the way the job caused me to size people up by how they might tip, was turning me into a person I didn't like.

I was ready for a change when I heard about the Mirage's management associate program, an entry-level track for employees interested in the corporate side. My application got me accepted into the advertising department, known internally as the "Toot Your Own Horn Department." Even though it meant a cut in pay to $17,500 a year, it seemed like a move in the right direction. I gave myself the title "Assistant Garbanzo Bean."

The department juggled dozens of projects, from newspaper and magazine ads to billboards and brochures. My job was to proof photos from different shoots. I sat at a light table every day and squinted through a loupe at hundreds of slides. It was easy work and left time to observe the others in the department. I saw the work people did and didn't do, the politics and the pecking order. The one thing I didn't see? Where I fit in.

But I wasn't about to leave. As with the tram, you never knew when an opportunity might appear, and so I practiced patience. One day, while wondering what might be next, I got a phone call, the first time that had happened in nearly six months of working there. Who would be calling for me? Assuming it was one of my friends, I said, "Hey, what's up?"

"Hello," a woman said. "I'm Jenny Delaney from William Morris."

I was so startled it wasn't one of my friends that I

didn't hear her clearly. I thought it was the cigarette company, Philip Morris.

"I think you have the wrong number," I said.

"No, I'm not with Philip Morris," she said. "I'm with the William Morris talent agency in Beverly Hills."

"Really?" I said.

"Yes."

She explained that she'd seen my friend Dustin Abraham perform several monologues, which, it turned out, I'd written, including the raw confessional "HR-7."

"Yes, that's mine," I said.

"I liked it," she said. "You have a voice, a strong voice. Have you ever written a screenplay?"

I felt like I was having an out-of-body experience. I'd spent years dreaming of having a conversation like this one. Unfortunately, I had to admit that I hadn't written a screenplay, which surprised her.

"Well, if you do write one and it's as good as the material you did for Dustin, I might like to represent you," she told me.

"That's great," I said. "I appreciate hearing that. It's really nice, really . . . nice."

I didn't know what else to say.

"Well, keep my name and number," she said. "If you write one, I'd definitely like to read it."

There was no question I was going to write a screenplay now. On my lunch break, I bought three books on screenwriting, starting with the primer of the profession, Syd Field's *Screenplay: The Foundations of Screenwriting—A*

Quick, Step-by-Step Guide from Concept to Finished Script. In it, he explains the basic three-act structure and character development, as well as the necessity of plot points, twists, conflict, and resolution. It was exactly what I needed—a crash course.

My favorite movies at the time included *The Deer Hunter*, the *Godfather* trilogy, *Jaws*, *GoodFellas*, all the other Scorsese films, *GoodFellas* again, *Midnight Cowboy*, *Kramer vs. Kramer*, and the entire Criterion collection. But when I thought about writing a film, *Pulp Fiction* and *Swingers*, two other recent classics, stood out as the kinds of movies I wanted to emulate. I heard those same sort of edgy, energetic voices in my head.

After finishing Field's book, I was ready to start. One crucial ingredient still eluded me, though—and that was an idea. I came up with dozens of my own and asked friends and family for suggestions, but it was Dustin who came up with the one that stuck. He said, "Dude, you should write something about a runner."

As soon as he said those words, *a runner*, I saw the movie; maybe not all of the individual parts and plot twists, but I saw the whole picture in my head and said, "That's exactly what I'm going to write."

Back in the summer when I was between ASU and UNLV, Dustin had worked as a runner for a rich gambler from Louisville, Kentucky. A runner was someone who went from casino to casino, looking for the best odds and phoning them to bookies and gamblers back east and in the Midwest. I spent the summer watching Dustin walk into casinos with a clipboard and a pocketful of quarters, jot down the lines, then call his guy from one of the pay phones that were always outside casinos and full of bookies.

The second Dustin mentioned a line that had good value, the guy would give him the bet—for instance, "five dimes on Green Bay"—and he would hang up and sprint to the counter. At times, Dustin ended the day with a hundred thousand or two hundred thousand dollars, which he delivered to a contact who supervised other runners. In Dustin's case, these drops were made at the Smith's Food King grocery store.

Despite the sums of money they handled, the runners themselves were paid very little and suffered consequences for mistakes. Dustin told me of one guy who lost a five-thousand-dollar ticket and had to pay for it. Another runner pocketed a few thousand; he was never heard from again.

In terms of a screenplay, I sensed this was a fresh, rich world. I'd seen a lot of movies, but none set in this arena, and none as I envisioned it.

Before writing, I researched the town for color and detail. I tried to look at the places and people with the curious eyes of a writer looking for characters and their stories. Who were the gamblers? The pit bosses? The pros? What had brought them there? Did they like their jobs? Were they honest? If not, why? What had happened? Who was the exhausted 21 dealer? What did a degenerate gambler look like? How did the people react when they were next to a winner? Who sat in the sports book all day? Why were all these people there?

By the time I was ready to write, I saw the whole movie in my head. The key had been figuring out my main character. I had to know his life, everything about him, and as I invented the details, I gave him a gambling addiction (which Dustin didn't have). Once I did that, I knew he would take a job with a mobster, he'd promise not to gamble, and inevitably he'd break that promise.

After work at the Mirage, I went to the UNLV library, parked myself in a carrel on the second floor, and wrote until the place closed. I went there weekends, too. Despite the long hours, it didn't seem like work. The action was so clear in my head that it was more like watching a movie than writing one. I couldn't wait to find out what would happen.

But not every hour was spent in front of my computer. One night, instead of pushing it till midnight, I met my friend Mike Bunin for a beer at Tom & Jerry's, a hangout near campus. Mike worked in UNLV's theater department and had read the script. Though I was eager to hear his opinion, I still complained about taking the night off when I could've been banging out a few more pages.

Mike held up his hand as if to say, "Stop." He said he had some notes and it might be good to talk and think about the story. He was right. But suddenly another story—a romance—took precedence. Before we got two steps inside the restaurant, I spotted Jennifer Brancucci at the end of the bar.

"Who's Jennifer?" Mike asked.

"Long story," I said.

"It looks like she's waiting for someone," he said.

"That makes talking to her even more urgent."

A year earlier, after living together for twenty years, my mom and David had gotten married. The wedding took place amid close friends at a tiny chapel, followed by dinner at the Bootlegger, a small Italian restaurant. As we enjoyed dinner, I spotted an attractive, dark-haired waitress across the restaurant. I was on my way to introduce myself when I saw it was Jennifer Brancucci, a girl I'd known slightly in high school. She had gotten even prettier.

We caught up, spent some time flirting, and toward the end of the night I suggested going out for a drink sometime. She seemed interested. When I asked if she was working the next night, she said she was, and I said, "Good, I'll get in contact with you." Later that night, I went to the store and bought her a friendship card. I took it to the restaurant the following evening, but she wasn't there. The manager said she'd been fired.

"Fired?" I said, confused. "I was here last night. I talked to her."

"It happened after you left."

"Can you give her this card?" I asked.

"I told you, she doesn't work here anymore," he said. "I don't know how to get in touch with her."

Now, twelve months later, Jennifer looked pained when I reminded her of that evening, but she didn't believe me when I said that I'd saved the card in case I ran into her again. Since I only lived a few minutes away, I told her that I'd prove it by getting the card. But I made her promise that she would wait at the restaurant for me, and she was there, smiling, when I returned with the card.

She opened the envelope, read the note, and pointed to the date. It was almost exactly a year later. What were the chances? The next night we went on our first date. Pretty soon we were inseparable. Independent in her own right, she accepted that I was work-oriented. She didn't try to change me. She understood the importance of my script and offered encouragement as I rounded the final turn.

In August 1996, I finished the script and braced for reaction. Dustin, who'd read pages every few days, thought I'd nailed it. So did Rico, who showed the script to his friend Anthony Manzo, who parked cars at Binion's casino. All of them took my writing seriously, and it meant a lot to have their support.

We were searching for our place in the world and the screenplay gave us a project around which we could rally and focus our dreams. We wanted to be rich and success-ful. We thought *The Runner* could be our ticket. The odds were against us, but when you grow up in Vegas you learn that long shots occasionally do pay off.

It happens.

36

Anthony Manzo said that his wife had a friend who was married to Mike Marvin, one of the producers of the low-budget 1984 teen ski comedy *Hot Dog . . . The Movie*. In May 1997, we met Mike at the Broadway Deli in Santa Monica. In his forties and with a ski bum's rugged good looks, he took command of the table, explaining that he had worked in TV and movies as a writer, director, and producer and knew the intricacies of the business. He warned that we weren't going to get *The Runner* made as fast as we thought, even if it was as good as we believed.

As we listened to him explain financing, distribution, direct-to-video, and foreign rights, it sounded as if it was almost impossible to get a movie made, and I sat at the table wondering if our six-hour drive through the desert had been a waste of time. He didn't sound encouraging, especially when he said, "Tony, you have no idea how many people out here have screenplays."

On the other hand, before we left, he took the script and promised to read it. I had no idea what to expect; at least we'd left on a hopeful note. As we said on the car ride back, Who knows—maybe he'll like it. And that's what happened. I was at work the following day when Mike called my cell phone.

"Kid, I read the script," he said.

"Yeah?"

"It's great," he said. "I want to make this movie."

"Really?" I said.

"I want to direct it," he continued. "I want you to meet my financial partner, too. When can you come back out?"

Rico, Manzo, and I returned to LA almost immediately, hooked up with Dustin, and met with Mike. He handed us off to Ron Moler, whose Aspect Ratio Films had produced a number of surf and ski movies. He saw *The Runner* as a mainstream film and he was very enthusiastic about its prospects.

Listening to him talk about developing the script further, whom he envisioned casting in the roles, and what he would do as the director was surreal. I had seen the picture in my head while writing the screenplay, but hearing someone with Ron's experience talk this enthusiastically took the whole project to another level, one that was beyond my comprehension. I suspected I had the same big, hungry grin that I saw on Dustin, Rico, and Manzo.

Finally, Ron switched gears and turned to business. He said he wanted to pay thirty-five thousand dollars for the rights to the film.

I couldn't say "Sold" fast enough.

That was huge money for something I created in a library carrel. But what sounded like a fortune would turn out to be a terrible business decision. What did I know? What did any of us know? We were as inexperienced as we had been told. Yet when I said we had a deal, not only did Ron shake my hand, he had me sit at his computer and write out a simple, straightforward deal memo.

"Just say we have a deal," he said. "Write that you are selling me *The Runner* for thirty-five thousand dollars."

Not a problem. Both Dustin and I, as co-registers on the script we had sent the Writers Guild, per the instructions in the how-to books, signed Ron's contract. Outside, the four of us celebrated, thinking we were about to take over Hollywood. For me, though, the best part was the validation. Someone in the business had recognized my talent as a creative individual, particularly as a writer.

At twenty-eight, it had taken me a long time to get to this point. But I finally felt like I had found myself as a writer. The next day I met with my boss and quit my job at the Mirage. She asked why.

"I sold a screenplay," I told her. "I'm moving to LA."

37

"What about me?" Jennifer asked, as we stood in my apartment.

"Once I get settled, you'll come join me," I said. "But first I need to start my career and focus on my work."

She didn't look happy. Jennifer was as eager as I was for a life beyond Las Vegas.

"You're not leaving me here," she said.

I didn't. Rico and I moved first. We rented a top-floor apartment at the Hollywood Tower on Franklin Avenue for $1,200 a month, which was way more than we could afford. Jennifer arrived soon after and leased an apartment in a mostly Spanish-speaking part of the city. We had no idea it was in the middle of gang-controlled turf. She was economical, and I was clueless.

I was ready to get to work on my movie. I expected Ron to cut a check and start production. Then reality kicked in. The process was excruciatingly slow and dependent on countless other people. Ron had a difficult time raising the money to actually make *The Runner*, and until he had enough cash in the bank, nothing happened other than the two of us meeting to talk about rewrites.

In the meantime, Rico and I, trying hard to fit into the Hollywood scene, ran through our money more rapidly than we had budgeted. Soon, instead of going out to eat, I was cruising the aisles at Smart & Final, where I left with a dozen jumbo cans of tomato sauce and about twenty pounds of pasta. I said if that ran out before we got paid, I was going back to Vegas.

Unbeknownst to me, a copy of *The Runner* ended up in front of Nancy Green-Keyes, a respected casting director. After reading it, she sent the script to David Seltzer, a manager at Addis Wechsler. He then gave it to his colleague Margaret Riley, who flipped for the material. At her firm's morning meeting, she told her coworkers it was one of the most original pieces of writing she had ever read. She just had one question: Who was this writer, Anthony Zuiker?

We agreed to meet at a café outside Beverly Hills on a summer day. It was close to 100 degrees outside. I arrived wearing a black turtleneck and slacks, the way I thought a serious writer should dress. As I walked in, I was perspiring so heavily I might as well have just stepped out of the shower. It was embarrassing when I introduced myself to Margaret: "Hello, I'm sweating profusely—but I'm not a weirdo. I'm just very hot."

Later, after we talked, she handed me a clean napkin to wipe the sweat on my forehead and said I didn't have to try to impress her. She was already impressed.

As I listened to her discuss my script, I felt the same way about her. Margaret was slight, with hazel eyes and shoulder-length hair. Her expertise about story and structure grew increasingly apparent as she dug deeper into *The*

Runner, and I found out her authority was genuine. After graduating from the American Film Institute, she worked in film production before shifting into management, and now she represented writers and directors.

"I love your writing," she said. "I love that you have a voice—an original voice that jumps off the page."

"I just write it the way I hear it," I said.

"Well, it's original, unique, and special, and that's going to get you noticed," she said.

Margaret agreed to represent me, and we shook hands at the table. I told her about my friends, Dustin, Rico, and Manzo, and explained that we wanted to work together on *The Runner* and other movies. She liked that we shared a dream. But she sounded a cautionary note. Getting assignments for a new writer would be hard enough, and that was going to be her focus. It would be even more difficult to bring along a *team* of new producers, too.

"We'll give it a shot and see what happens," I said, and my friends agreed.

Soon Margaret had me meet with all the major agencies, but in my head I knew Creative Artists Agency was the best and I wanted to be there. My meeting with them was last. It was set up for lunch at Barney Greengrass.

I waited in a booth for thirty minutes before calling Margaret to ask if the two agents from CAA, David Styne and Scott Greenberg, were running late.

"What do you mean?" she said, alarmed. "They called me fifteen minutes ago. They're waiting for you in the restaurant."

"I don't see any agents here," I said.

"Where are you?"

"Barney's," I said.

"Greengrass?"

"No. Beanery," I said. "Barney's Beanery." The difference between the two places is extreme. One is a fancy deli in Beverly Hills catering to agents in thousand-dollar suits and the other is in West Hollywood and boasts an unparalleled selection of beer.

"You're at the wrong one," she said.

"Oh God."

"Don't panic," she said. "Let me take care of it."

The meeting was rescheduled for the next day at the Peninsula hotel, where David and Scott took over a corner table at the bar. After laughing about my mistake, they asked me about growing up in Las Vegas, and that led naturally to a discussion about *The Runner*, which they said was very strong—strong enough that they could see signing me as a client.

"But we need something else," Scott said.

I hadn't heard that in previous meetings. Hoping I didn't look surprised, I cocked my head and asked, "What do you mean?"

"We'd like to see another sample of your writing," he said.

I took a sip of water and thought about how to respond. I didn't have another sample. I knew the one I had was good and that I was capable of writing another script of similar if not better quality. But my future was now. I was broke and didn't want to have to go back to Vegas and look for a job.

I quickly thought about what I could say to keep them interested. I didn't have many options. I decided the truth was my best hope, and so I rolled the dice, Vegas-style.

"This script is all I got," I told them. "Either sign me or don't sign me."

Everything I had was on the table. I didn't expect a decision then. I thought either David or Scott would tell me that they had to go back to the office and confer with their department. But they turned out to be gamblers, too. David reached out to shake my hand, and Scott said, "We're in."

Jennifer had found a job waitressing in the coffee shop at the Beverly Hills Hotel, where her regulars included Ozzy and Sharon Osbourne, and I waited until she got off work and came over before telling her the good news. When she asked how the meeting had gone, I opened the kitchen cabinet and gestured toward the cans of tomato sauce and boxes of pasta sitting on the shelves. I hadn't run out yet.

"I'm still in the game," I said.

38

Since Ron was having trouble raising money for *The Runner*, my agents asked him to relinquish some of the control he had over the picture. They said he would still participate as a producer if it sold elsewhere, but they asked him to give up his right to direct. It seemed like such an obvious decision that my team went ahead and sent the script out to production companies, expecting Ron to agree and let them handle the heavy lifting of selling the picture.

Then two things happened.

First, Sony Pictures liked *The Runner*. They called my agents with a mind-blowing two-picture deal, offering six figures for *The Runner* and another six figures for a second "blind" script to be written later. I nearly passed out when Margaret and my agents explained that I could make more than a million dollars if both movies got made. I was still eating pasta and ketchup sandwiches.

But then Ron refused to relinquish his right to direct. He reminded everyone that he had a signed contract. He owned the project. I saw my million-dollar fantasy disappear.

"He only paid thirty-five thousand dollars," I complained to Margaret and my agents.

"But he paid it," she explained. "He has a contract."

I was sick.

"What's the story behind that contract again?" David asked.

"He had me type it up in his office," I said.

"And you signed it?"

"I did."

"From now on, never sign anything without—"

"You don't have to say it," I interrupted. "I learned my lesson."

If that left a bad taste, it was short-lived. In late 1997, Ron finally rounded up enough money to start production. We filmed in Utah with a cast of recognizable names led by Ron Eldard, who starred as the compulsive gambler running bets for a mobster played by John Goodman. Courteney Cox and Joe Mantegna also starred. Goodman paid me a big compliment when he said my writing reminded him of the wonderful Coen brothers.

I was disappointed the movie wasn't the big-budget feature I had envisioned, but I was happy being on the set, surrounded by creative people. I pounded out rewrites as needed and ran lines with Courteney several times. I got involved whether someone wanted an opinion or needed help moving a piece of equipment.

I was philosophic about the way things had played out. If Sony had bought *The Runner*, they probably would have brought in another writer to rewrite the picture and I never would have gotten near the set. I felt just as fortunate when Ron included me in postproduction. I was getting an education. Even when Ron couldn't get a distributor, which meant the movie went straight to Blockbuster, I remained upbeat—I had a premiere in my living room.

Later, someone asked what I thought of the movie. "Who watched the movie?" I said. "I got as far as the credits and then hit the pause button when I saw 'Written by Anthony Zuiker.' I didn't need to watch any more."

As far as I was concerned, that was the best part.

39

I may not have been heading back to Las Vegas, but I was still broke and looking for work. Margaret and my agents were sending me out on interviews for prospective writing assignments all the time, and it became apparent to Rico and Manzo that we all weren't going to make it as we had dreamed. I was pitching my heart out, but it was impossible to also attach a bunch of new producers to movies that already had producers.

Disappointed, Rico and Manzo returned to Vegas and rethought their careers while Dustin remained in LA and focused on acting. In the long run, it was the right move for everyone. I stayed, hoping for the best, but I also felt the reality of impending desperation. I wasn't stupid. For a few hours, I nearly had a million dollars. Now I had next to nothing. This was going to be a test of faith.

One night, needing to get out of the apartment, I went to Barney's Beanery to work on some material. I ordered a pitcher of beer and a pot of coffee, something I had seen Quentin Tarantino do when he was writing *From Dusk Till Dawn*. He also wrote *Pulp Fiction* there.

Unfortunately, I also had to pay the check. When the waitress brought my bill, I wasn't able to come up with the twenty-eight dollars I owed. She returned my debit card, offering a sympathetic "Sorry, it was declined," and then asked what else I wanted to use.

Except I didn't have anything else. I explained that my debit card was all I had. The waitress told me to think about it while she took care of some other tables. I figured the best plan was to go to Dustin's house and borrow thirty bucks. So I got up and told the waitress I was going to my friend's place.

"I'll be right back," I said. "He lives pretty close."

As I moved past her, though, she must have signaled the bouncer, a burly dude with biceps splitting the seams of his flannel shirt. When I got to the door, he grabbed my shoulder and squeezed. I froze.

"Dude, where you going?" he asked.

"My friend's house," I said. "I'm going to get some cash. I'll be right back."

"What's going to guarantee I see you again?" he asked.

Back when I was a bellman, and the tips were flowing, I had bought myself an expensive Panerai watch. I handed it to the bouncer. I couldn't believe this was happening to me. It was like a scene from a bad movie.

"See ya," he said.

Outside, I got halfway down the block before remembering that Dustin was out of town. I slumped against the window of a furniture store and put my head in my hands. I had no idea what to do. For the next ten minutes, I just sat there. It was one of the few times in my life I didn't have a clue about what to do. I thought about saying, "Screw it," and leaving my fifteen-hundred-dollar watch at Barney's Beanery while I went home and rethought my life.

I couldn't believe I was almost thirty-one years old and unable to pay a twenty-eight-dollar bar tab. Pathetic.

Desperate, I swallowed my pride and phoned Margaret. She showed up in front of the restaurant twenty minutes later. After a reassuring pat on the shoulder, she paid the bill and returned with my watch.

"It happens," she said. "Keep your chin up."

It was hard. For a while, I survived on the deli platters, sandwiches, and soup that Margaret and CAA sent over out of concern that I might truly starve. Most of the time I was able to convince myself these lean times were only a test and I'd come out the other end. Other times I thought I was nuts to think I could make a living in Hollywood. Margaret's pep talks helped.

One day she called with promising news. She had been at Sony and found a project that seemed as though it had been waiting for me. It was a rewrite of a script about the Harlem Globetrotters.

A sports story?

I loved it.

However, as I knew, every great sports story goes beyond sports, and the Globetrotters were far more than just a basketball team. The bones of the film had been in the original draft. It was set in the 1940s and 1950s, about twenty years after the team was founded, and it focused on the relationship between the team's five-foot-two owner, Abe Saperstein, and its six-foot-two player-coach, Inman Jackson.

Saperstein and Jackson, a savvy Jew and a proud, smart, strong, gifted black man, were headstrong and ambitious. Both knew the painful frustrations of discrimination and hate, yet both refused to be victims of it. They were an unlikely pair who never would have come into contact if not for the Globetrotters. As it was, though, they needed each other. On and off the court, their battles with each other paled next to their real fight against the world.

Margaret was right. It was my kind of story: emotional, dramatic, full of opportunity, and something I hadn't seen before.

"How do I get the job?" I asked.

"Sony loves your work," Margaret said. "Go in and pitch them."

"How much does it pay?" I asked.

"Get the job, and then we'll make the deal," she said.

Within a few weeks, I was buried in research, and then CAA and Margaret received an offer for me to write the sequel to *I Know What You Did Last Summer*. The original, starring Jennifer Love Hewitt, had been a box office hit, and this sequel was already green-lit. It was being fast-tracked into theaters. In fact, the producer had already hired another writer to crank out a rewrite in addition to the one I was being offered.

It was a classic bake-off. The producers would pick the script they liked best or perhaps hire a new writer to harvest bits from both.

Either way, I was guaranteed the film would get made and my name would be on the screen in theaters the following summer. I was also assured of getting paid a lot of money: three hundred thousand dollars.

"How much will the Globetrotters pay?" I asked Margaret again.

"First, you have to get the job," she said. "But it will be about what a first-time writer gets."

"How much is that?" I asked.

"Around a hundred thousand," she said. "Think about what you want to do."

What was there to think about? I could get paid three hundred thousand dollars for a movie that was certain to get made or I could gamble on getting the Globetrotters writing job, and get paid much less. Where was the debate? I wanted to take the sure thing, the sequel to *I Know What You Did Last Summer.* I think ninety-nine out of a hundred people would have done the same thing.

The one exception?

My manager.

At a meeting in her office, Margaret advised me to turn down the guaranteed money and try to get the Harlem Globetrotters gig. She said the thing that had originally attracted her to my writing was my voice. It was original, raw, and energetic—it stood out. If I wrote a horror sequel, she said, I would have to make it sound like the first one, which meant stifling my voice, my creativity, and everything else that made me unique.

"Is that worth it?" she asked.

"But the money," I said. "It's huge."

"It is a lot," she said. "But I'm thinking about your

career, and I don't think taking the sequel is a good career move."

I had already missed out on the potential six or seven figures *The Runner* might've earned me. Now I was seeing another six-figure deal pass me by. I understood Margaret's rationale. I even agreed with it. I just couldn't quite bring myself to utter those words. I mean, who passed up that kind of money?

"So you're telling me not to do it," I said.

"I'm recommending that you go for the better, more literary project," she said. "It's a project you can write with your heart, and your voice will come through on every page. I think that will do more for your career."

"What about the money?" I asked.

"Don't worry about the money," she said. "Just write something great. The money will come."

"What if it doesn't?"

"It will."

"But what if it doesn't?"

"Anthony, don't worry."

"I'm broke."

"We'll set up the meeting."

40

Whether it was superstition or just good work habits, I had to arrive early. For my 10:30 meeting at Sony, I showed up at 7:30 a.m. and went straight to the commissary, where I commandeered a table in the back, got out my note cards, and practiced my pitch. I was a stickler for regimen and rehearsal. I wanted every beat of my presentation imprinted on my brain.

Obsessive? Unquestionably. At eight, Margaret called my cell, asking why I was already at the studio. She had gotten an email from an executive who was going to be in our meeting later. He had seen me in the commissary and worried there was a scheduling mistake. Now Margaret was concerned.

There was no mistake, I told her. I just wanted the job.

The meeting with a half dozen of Sony's top executives couldn't have gone better. Following a round of introductions, I described my vision and then engaged in a spirited question-and-answer session that confirmed they approved of my take on the Globetrotters project. Actually, at the end, there was little doubt I was the right man for the job. The executive in charge came right out and asked, "When can you start?"

I looked around as if it were a trick question.

"When I get the job," I said.

Over the next sixteen months, I would write numerous drafts. I worked with the different producers attached to the project, each of whom had their own notes, their own ideas, and their own suggestions for the story. It was part of the moviemaking process, as I discovered: If you couldn't work in a group situation, then Hollywood wasn't the right place for you. With Margaret's support, I not only navigated the process, but I managed to hang on to the core elements of my script, which involved the complicated relationship between Saperstein and Jackson.

Sometimes as I wrote, I found myself thinking about Eddie for the first time in years. It was the material. It caused painful emotions I had shut off for my own protection to surface again. Now that I was an adult, I understood them more, and they hurt less. I was resigned that we would lead our separate lives, though deep down, sometimes when I stared at the computer screen, Saperstein and Jackson became Eddie and myself—I saw how closely tied we were.

It wasn't a revelation; it was more of a reality check. Like it or not, my dad's influence was indelible. He had made me want to not end up like him. When people asked about my compulsive work habits, I didn't explain. It would have taken too long and been too personal. But it was all Eddie.

When he suddenly popped back into my life, I had little desire to speak to him. I had just asked Jennifer to marry me, and we had gone to Vegas to share the good news with our families. There, I spotted Eddie. It was Saturday afternoon, and I'd walked into the Vacation Village casino and was adjusting to the chaos when I saw him nearby, heading toward the exit. I sensed he had seen me and wanted to get away.

Before he could leave, I walked over and said hello, with an awkward hug that made Eddie take a step back. He had heard from my mom that I was working in Hollywood and asked how that was going. He hadn't heard the news about Jennifer yet. I told him in part so he would know, but also to see if he would show any interest in my life. He didn't. The encounter lasted a few minutes before Eddie said he had to go. We shook hands, and I watched him exit the casino and disappear down the sidewalk. He never turned back to look.

On April 11, 1998, Jennifer and I were married in an outdoor ceremony in Las Vegas. Her large Italian family filled the aisles, and my stepdad, David, stood in as my best man. Dustin, Rico, and Manzo were all there, too.

But on our return to LA, we were greeted by bad news. Sony didn't want to make the Globetrotters movie. After countless rewrites and suggestions from all the producers, they didn't think it was commercial enough.

On the bright side, everyone said they liked my work. My writing was top-notch. But the compliments didn't take away the disappointment. Frustrated and in need of a break from the business, Jennifer and I moved back to Vegas. She wanted to be closer to her family, and I thought that putting some distance between Hollywood and myself would help me recharge.

At the end of summer in 1998, Jennifer got pregnant and suddenly I had plenty of motivation. Margaret and

CAA had me flying to LA for lots of meetings, including one with Leonardo DiCaprio for a project about young gangsters called *Hoodfellas*. It was based on a magazine story about these ruthless kids who had new-school mob rules.

I thought I was going to walk in and find a polished movie star. Instead, Leo was at his desk, wearing shorts, a T-shirt, and a baseball cap. He had a half-eaten bagel in front of him. I grabbed a Diet Coke from the fridge, tossed him a can, and acted out half the movie. I played every part. I did all the voices, characters, sound effects. I was a maniac.

And Leo ate it up. When I finished, he gave me a big hug and said, "You've got the job."

But it didn't go anywhere.

As often happens in the movies, he decided on another project after I had finished a draft. After that, the producers Art and John Linson hired me to work on their skateboarding feature, *Lords of Dogtown*. Meanwhile, as I worked on the movie scripts, Margaret suggested I think about television.

Between networks and cable, some excellent series were being made, including *NYPD Blue*, *Law & Order: Special Victims Unit*, *The Practice*, *Ally McBeal*, and *The Sopranos*. All of these shows, she pointed out, shared a common ingredient—strong writing.

Margaret thought the networks would respond to my voice. She had me meet with the CAA TV agent Joe Cohen, another fan of *The Runner*. Joe knew more about TV than anyone I'd ever met, and he knew it from the inside out. He gave me an in-depth tutorial on the way TV worked, starting with the business of TV. He wanted me to understand the way decisions were made. Then he focused on the creative side, explaining how ideas were developed and owned.

Each example he provided led to the same place: Great TV began with great writing. Writing is what got TV shows off the ground, and what enabled them to endure. He provided numerous examples, from *Your Show of Shows* to *Hill Street Blues*. What was the common denominator? Exceptional writing. What made exceptional writing? A unique way of looking at the world, an original voice. He mentioned *The Runner* and said that if I came up with an idea for TV, I should set it in Las Vegas.

"You ooze Vegas from every pore in your body," he said. "The voice will be there if you write about what you know."

As for ideas, he suggested picking a template that had been successful on TV in the past and paying homage to it. He pointed out that David Lynch and Mark Frost had remade *Peyton Place* into *Twin Peaks*. He told me to read pilots, watch TV, go to the Museum of Television to watch old shows, and find a format that I liked and then update it.

"Give it a new take, a new twist," he said. "Give it Anthony Zuiker."

He also said he wanted to set up a meeting for me in LA with Jonathan Littman, the president of Jerry Bruckheimer Television. Jonathan had read my Globetrotters script and had asked to meet with me.

"Are they looking for anything in particular?" I asked.

"Don't worry about that," Joe said. "Just go in and meet Jonathan. Talk about whatever's exciting to you."

41

It wasn't exactly an idea . . . yet.

But one afternoon I was on my way outside to play basketball with the kid next door. I stopped to put the air in the ball. Jennifer, six months pregnant, asked me to stay in and watch TV with her instead. I glanced outside. I looked forward to playing one-on-one with our neighbor's son. He was sixteen, a foot taller than me, and I usually kicked his ass. Few things made me happier.

"What's on?" I asked.

"It's some show on Discovery," she said. "It's called *The New Detectives*. It looks pretty good."

"How about recording it?" I asked. "We'll watch it later."

"No," she said. "Come sit down and watch it with me."

I'd spent all day in front of a computer. I felt like some exercise. I felt like kicking the neighbor kid's ass.

"Come on, babe," she said.

OK, I'd get the kid next time. I put the ball down, sat next to my wife, and from then on my life was never the same. *The New Detectives* was a docudrama about police investigators who employed state-of-the-art science to solve cold cases. The production quality was very MTV—quick cuts, gritty, lots of backtracking into the story. I was hooked in the first five minutes.

This particular episode was about Linda Sobek, a former Oakland Raiders cheerleader turned model-and-actress who'd been murdered by a photographer assigned to take her picture. All the elements worked. It was exciting TV.

One scene in particular jumped out at me. It was when investigators pulled a hair follicle from the passenger-side headrest in the photographer's car and laid it on a piece of paper that they put under a microscope. They saw the hair was still attached to the seed—usually an indication of struggle, they explained.

"They can tell all that from a hair follicle?" I said. "Wow."

"This is great, isn't it?" Jennifer said. "It's a whole different way of solving crimes—at least it is to me. If there was a cop show like this, I'd watch."

Jump to the following week. I was in LA, meeting with Jonathan Littman. It was what Hollywood refers to as "a general." He gave me an overview of the Bruckheimer company, and I let him get to know me. The hope was that we'd click and set up a second meeting. But we did more than click. As we discussed the kinds of shows we watched and liked, we segued naturally into a conversation about ideas, and all of a sudden I found myself riffing about forensic investigators who used the latest scientific tools to solve crimes.

"Say you walk in to a crime scene," I said. "There's a woman on the kitchen floor, dead. There's a plant knocked over and a pink elephant in the backyard. We know what happened. What we don't know is how it happened, who did it, or why. But science can unravel the mystery."

"It's a cop show?" Jonathan said.

"Yeah, but with science," I said. "And a great look. It would be graphic, high-tech, and cool. Like a Bruckheimer movie on TV."

"Tell me about the science," he said.

"The cops are like scientists," I said. "They're forensic criminologists. And in terms of telling the story, it would use flashbacks, cool editing, and lots of special effects. It'd be a whole new kind of cop show."

Jonathan liked it.

"Do you have anything written up?" he asked.

"No," I said. "Not yet."

As meetings went, it was a home run. But Jonathan let me know a lot of work had to be done to prepare a pitch that the company would take to the networks. After all, Jerry Bruckheimer had produced *Top Gun*, *The Rock*, and *Con Air*—he was known for having exceptionally high standards, and as Jonathan said, that standard was even higher within their offices. But Jonathan was on board if I wanted to develop the idea. I did, indeed.

First, Jonathan had me watch several movies to get a better sense of different ways to tell stories and develop characters. After I watched them, he encouraged me to do research, to spend time in the field and talk to actual crime scene investigators. As he explained, if I was going to create a series that would run for years, I had to understand these people personally as well as professionally. In fact, Jerry Bruckheimer himself came into the room for that part of the discussion and emphasized that element.

"Take some guys out and get them drinking," he said. "Order some bottles of wine, and listen to them talk about what they do. That's where you're going to find the stories that will tell you whether you have a series."

Back in Vegas, I received permission from the Las Vegas Police Department's Public Affairs office to observe CSIs in the field-services division. The department's rules allowed visitors to spend only eight hours with officers in the field during any one calendar year. That was one shift, not enough time to learn the kind of intimate details I wanted.

But I had barely stepped into the CSI office when I spotted Monte Spoor, a guy I had known in high school. He gave me the same look that I gave him: What the hell are you doing here?

It turned out Monte was a senior crime scene analyst. After hearing my intentions, he introduced me to his colleagues and arranged for me to ride along that night. That evening, I saw the aftermath of a couple of small robberies and chatted with some cops. But it didn't even begin to scratch the surface of my needs. My notebook was still empty. So Monte spoke to his boss and cleared the way for me to return the next day.

I ended up tagging along for about five weeks.

42

The Las Vegas crime lab was housed in an unassuming office building on West Charleston Boulevard. Monte shared an office with twenty-year veteran Daniel Holstein, the dean of the department. When I walked through the door on my second day, I met Daniel, who asked me to check out his desk. I walked over to where he sat and he opened the top drawer. I looked in and saw vials of maggots. I almost vomited.

Not fazed, he asked if he could take a pint of my blood.

"Why do you want a pint of my blood?" I asked.

Daniel turned around and opened a small refrigerator filled with pints of blood. He was one of a handful of people in the country licensed in blood-splatter analysis, and he wanted to use my blood to practice castoff analysis in his basement over the weekend.

"That's what you do on the weekend?" I asked.

Daniel smiled, though not ghoulishly. But yes, it's what he did—and he was damn good at it.

"When you hit someone in the head with a crowbar or any kind of blunt object, the first hit is free," he said. "There's no blood."

I jotted that down on my notepad.

"The first hit causes the laceration," he continued.

"Then the blood starts, so the second hit absorbs blood and that's when you get the castoff, the blood flinging across the floor and on the wall."

"All right." I nodded. "I get it."

"So roll up your sleeve," he said.

"No."

"Sure?" he asked.

"It's a hell of an offer," I said, laughing nervously. "But no thanks."

There's a variation of that exact scene in the *CSI* pilot. When Grissom is seen for the first time, he's asking Holly Gribbs, a new officer, to roll up her sleeve. "I need a pint of your blood," he says. "It's customary for all new hires." Gribbs later refuses his offer of something to eat. "I don't want to eat anything that's been in this office," she says. "Is there a grasshopper in here?"

It all came from Daniel. His approach to the work came to define the entire series: *Concentrate on what cannot lie—the evidence.*

Grissom actually said that to Warrick Brown (Gary Dourdan), adding, "There is no room in this department for subjectivity. You know that, Warrick. We handle every case objectively and without presupposition, regardless of race, color, creed, or bubble-gum flavor."

That material all came from my time with Daniel. And so did other material that ended up in the show. A woman ran the lab, which had cops looking through microscopes, working with DNA, and running ballistics reports. And I met an investigator who had worked for thirty-six hours straight, searching for prints in an armored truck that had been hijacked, and I saw him practically freak out with excitement when he found a single print on a sliver of duct tape.

I also met Yolanda McCleary, a ranking CSI. A single mother of two, she was a sexy brunette who was also brilliant. She more than held her own in this male-dominated environment, and she became the inspiration for Marg Helgenberger's character, Catherine Willows.

Just as Jerry and Jonathan had predicted, the time I spent hanging out with the real CSIs paid off. I was out with them one night when we came across the bodies of a young tattooed guy and his sixteen-year-old girlfriend. I remarked on how innocent they both looked. One of the CSIs glanced over at me and shook his head.

"If you're walking around at two in the morning, chances are you aren't that innocent," he said.

That same night we stopped at a 7-Eleven after it had been robbed. As the CSIs dusted the counter and doors and checked the surveillance footage, the traumatized store owner, a short Indian woman, recounted to me what had happened. I listened, but told her I wasn't a cop. Hearing that I was a Hollywood writer, she asked if I wanted to buy her store.

"No thanks," I said.

"Why not?"

"Why not?" I said, trying not to laugh. "You just got robbed."

Later that week, the cops let me tag along as they

busted a handful of crystal meth labs. The labs doubled as homes where people lived in extreme squalor. I gagged when I walked into the first one. After a few, I saw that they all looked the same. Clothes, pots and pans, dirty dishes, children's toys were all strewn on the floor, and roaches crawled over everything, like workers in a junkyard. I felt layers of scum under my feet.

They all had another common feature: beer bottle caps pushed into the ceiling. I never figured out why. The cops had no explanation, either.

"This place is awful," I said in one house. "I can't believe people live this way."

The CSI next to me shook his head.

"Wait till you go into some of the places where they die," he said.

43

I walked through the front door of my house at about six in the morning, dirty and drained. I sat at the kitchen table and wrote notes. I was still writing when Jennifer woke up and asked how it had gone. "Terrifying and sensational," I told her, adding that it was a war zone out there—drugs, murder, and depravity. None of us knew anything about it because none of it ever made the news.

"I was sick to my stomach the whole night," I said. "I was scared to death. Bad things happened. It was unimaginable."

"Don't go back," Jennifer said. "You'll get killed. It's not worth it."

Not worth it? I was getting great material. Neither fear nor fatigue would get in my way.

One night, we were in the middle of the shift when a call crackled over the radio. A guy had bought it in a house that had been engulfed in flames during the gunfire. As we pulled in front of the fire-ravaged house, my instinct was that it had been a meth lab explosion. I was starting to think like a cop. Inside, we found a dead guy with a huge gash through his forehead where an air conditioner had fallen from the second-floor roof and sliced into him. If he hadn't died from gunshot wounds or the fire, his last breath came when that chunk of his head went out.

I followed the body from the crime scene to the coroner's office, where I met forensic pathologist Dr. Gary Telgenhoff. He let me watch as he opened up the guy's chest cavity with a Y incision and showed me the ribs, which, as he observed, were well done from the fire. The stench wafting up from the man's chest made me sick, and I waited outside.

Afterward, Dr. T took me into the missing persons' cooler, a room with a wall of drawers holding people from the streets and other locals who had died and gone unidentified. In another room, he showed me two teenagers, a boy, seventeen, and a girl, sixteen. They had been killed in a head-on collision on their way to Vegas from LA. He surmised that they had been on their way to elope.

"What made you think that?" I asked.

"The boy had a ring in his pocket," he said.

"She's beautiful—Winona Ryder, but still a teenager," I said. "I don't even see a mark on her."

Dr. T lifted her head slightly and moved it around a bit, just enough to let me see that everything had been severed on impact. He also pointed out the marks that the shoulder straps had left on their bodies. I immediately began to wonder who their parents were, what their lives were like, what they had done to cause these two kids to sneak off to get married. And what would it be like when they received the news of the car wreck?

A few nights later, I was at Caesars Palace with a

couple of CSIs. It was 3 a.m., and we were eating lunch. One investigator ordered lobster bisque, and the other had a plate of Chinese food with a side of fried rice. They were talking about an ex-gangbanger they had found after he'd been dead a few days. They used the rice to illustrate maggots coming out of his body.

What was it with these guys? How could they be so casual about something so awful?

On another occasion, I was in a car with a sergeant from the Vegas PD when a call came on the radio for help. Officers were in pursuit on foot about three miles away from where we were. The sergeant hit the accelerator, flipped on the lights and siren, and we took off through the city like a missile, blowing through traffic, red lights, and anything else in our way.

I had never been more scared in my life. From the way we were speeding across town, it seemed like guaranteed death. I wanted to ask him to let me out, slow down, or at least look both ways as he went through intersections, but I was even more scared of seeming scared. I prayed we would just survive.

At last, we screeched to a stop. Safely. I saw several cops leaping over a wall and another running down the street as they pursued the perp. My sergeant hopped out of the car and joined the chase, yelling at me to stay put. I didn't move. I felt like a six-year-old locked in the car while his mom ran into the store. Minutes later, they brought out the dogs.

They didn't find the suspect, but they did find his beeper.

There was some talk about what to do with it. Then a Latina female officer scrolled through the numbers and got on her phone.

"Yo, yo, yo, where the party at, yo?" she said. "Where the party at?"

She listened to the response, then smiled.

"We are just kind of chillin' over here . . . We hear you guys got a party . . . Where you at? Tell me and I'll be over."

Her act was gangster—and effective. She got the address of the motel where the guy and his friends were holed up. A few minutes later, I was in one of six cop cars that arrived at the motel and arrested three people. But it turned out that the suspect they had chased earlier had left and gone to another house—our next stop. He was taken into custody there.

I was fascinated by how the officers followed one lead after another until they finished the job. "Follow the facts," I wrote in my notepad. "Let the facts talk to you."

Another night, I went on a sexual assault call. A nineteen-year-old girl had seduced another nineteen-year-old girl at a club and taken her back to a motel where three men who were waiting in the room raped her. When we showed up, several other cops had the suspects in custody and investigators were gathering evidence in the room. The victim had already been taken away in protective custody, but the cops couldn't find the girl who had lured her there.

I followed the CSIs under the crime scene tape and

went inside. After a moment or two, one of the investigators told me to "glove up" and search around the bed for "biologicals." Prior to my research, I thought cops were a one-stop shop, doing everything from making arrests to gathering evidence. I was unaware of the specialists who appeared on the scene after a suspect was in custody. It was a full operation including plainclothes officers, detectives, scientists, and now an evidence-gathering writer.

" 'Biologicals'?" I said. "You mean hair?"

He shook his head.

"Semen, you dummy."

I watched as he took pictures, folded up the bedsheets, and put them in a bag. Then I felt the bed move. For a second, I thought it was the CSI hitting it with his knee. Then it moved again. But he had already stepped away. I bent down, lifted the bed skirt, and saw two red eyes staring back at me like a feral cat in the dark. It was her—the girl they were looking for.

With lightning speed, she reached up and scratched my face. I screamed as I recoiled.

"Under the bed!" I yelled. "Someone's under the bed!"

Three cops instantly stood the bed up, grabbed the girl by her ankles, and yanked her backward about ten feet. Their guns were already drawn as they told her to "freeze!"

I was ready to piss my pants.

"Don't shoot me!" I yelled. "I'm just the writer."

Later, outside, I realized I had seen enough. It was

time to stop. I had accumulated several books of notes, character sketches, and stories. I felt the same way I did before I wrote *The Runner*. My head was full of people and stories. I heard the characters speaking in my head. Now they wanted to get out, and I needed to let them out. I couldn't wait to start my treatment, to get something on paper. I was, in fact, making the last of my notes when that girl under the bed was taken outside and put into the back of a patrol car.

"Anthony, when are you coming back?" one of the CSIs asked.

"You know what?" I said. "I'm good. I'm ready to write."

"Great to hear. I hope you got what you needed," he said. "Best of luck with your TV show."

PART VII

PRIME TIME

44

It was early October when Jonathan and I were ready to sell the show. As prepared as we were, though, we didn't make it easy on ourselves. The window for pitching began in midsummer and ended in the fall. We were late, and most of the networks were already done with the process, including NBC and Fox. Neither wanted to hear the pitch. ABC let us come in, but they quickly passed. That left one network, CBS.

We were able to get a meeting with Nina Tassler, the CBS senior vice president of drama development. But just before we entered her office, Jonathan stopped me.

"It's only going to be Nina in the room," he said.

I puzzled over that one. Network meetings weren't like that.

"You mean this isn't ten people in a conference room, waiting for my performance?" I asked.

"No," he said, and with a wicked smile, he added, "Also, keep in mind since all the other networks are either closed or have passed, if you don't sell the show here it's dead, or it's midseason. So, no pressure."

"That's your pep talk?" I said.

He nodded.

"Fantastic," I said. "Let's do it."

Nina couldn't have been more polite when Jonathan introduced me, but I assumed she was merely taking the meeting out of respect to the Bruckheimer company. Ordinarily, four or five network executives attended pitch meetings, each with his or her own input and authority, and even though Nina was CBS's top creative executive, I still interpreted the low turnout as a sign that our show wasn't much of a priority.

It affected my energy. Instead of one of my trademark animated pitches where I acted out all the parts, I took off my glasses, shut my eyes, and in a slow, deliberate tone of voice matter-of-factly described the show.

"It's called *CSI: Crime Scene Investigation*," I began. "It's about a group of science nerd cops who go to crime scenes, scrutinize the evidence, piece it back together, and by the end bring peace of mind to the survivors. The main character is Gil Grissom. He's an enigmatic thinker. He specializes in blood-splatter analysis. He eats chocolate-covered crickets. He doesn't care what people say. He just follows the evidence . . ."

I spoke for about fifteen minutes. When I finished, I let out a huge gust of air, a giant exhale that said, "Well, that's it. That's what I've got." Then I looked at Nina. The dark-haired CBS executive was smiling.

"That's an amazing pitch," she said.

"Really?" I said, glancing at Jonathan with surprise.

"You know, we're going younger this year," she said. "We're doing a new show called *Survivor*. If you write me a great pilot, I'll go upstairs to Leslie [CBS president and

CEO Leslie Moonves] and fight for it. I think the show is exactly what this network needs."

She turned to Jonathan.

"I love it," she said. "I'll buy it."

I don't know if anything else was said after that—if there was additional conversation, I didn't hear it. I was in a daze until Jonathan and I stepped in the elevator. As soon as the doors shut, I freaked out. I couldn't believe what had just happened. She *loved* it. She was going to buy my show. Jonathan slapped me on the back.

"Yes, that's how you do it, my friend!" he said. "That's how you sell it in the room!"

45

Over the next few days, I had several more conversations with Jonathan and Nina, whose faith in my ability as a new, untested writer never wavered. In a way, it reminded me of the woman from Hallmark who had years earlier acknowledged my talent and encouraged me to persevere. Then I returned to Vegas, commandeered a carrel at the UNLV library, and spent the next week writing the *CSI* pilot.

I had rehearsed the opening scene so many times in my head and practiced pitching it that finally writing it was like taking dictation. I began with Grissom investigating a suicide that turned out to be a homicide. I included flashbacks, science, sex, violence, and descriptions more graphic than anything then on prime time. At the end of each day, I sent pages to Jonathan and he emailed me back comments—though not many—and encouragement. The network reacted similarly. Nina and her team were very positive. I felt the forces aligning behind the project until it took on a life of its own.

Nina thought *CSI* could be a strong addition to CBS's lineup, and she provided the most crucial step by arranging for me to meet with William Petersen. If a series is going to a) get on the air, and b) have a chance at being a hit, it needs a star, and Billy was a star—a strong, handsome, Steppenwolf-trained actor known for the movies *To Live and Die in L.A.* and *Manhunter*.

He had a deal with CBS, but he hadn't yet found a series. The network believed in him, though, in his power to attract an audience. If he said yes to *CSI*, we had a shot at getting on the air. My wife went a step further. She declared that if he said yes, we had a hit.

Billy and I met at the Four Seasons Hotel in Beverly Hills. I arrived with Jonathan, and Billy brought his manager and producing partner, Cynthia Chvatal. But it was he and I who talked. We zeroed in on each other's backgrounds and connected over his hometown Chicago Cubs, and our mutual appreciation of a fine beer.

When it came time to discuss the show, I brought out a copy of the script. He had already read it, and we talked about the concept. I didn't know if there was protocol, so I pitched him hard on the idea. It led to an intense and detailed conversation about his potential character, Grissom. Before we left, he turned to his manager and said, "I like it. I'm in. This is the one I want to do."

CBS called Billy afterward and asked him about several other projects they thought suited him. They wanted him to be sure before he committed to *CSI*. The network wanted to be sure, too. He stood by his decision. He had a vision as strong as mine. He wanted to play Gil Grissom and make *CSI* a great show.

And from that moment on, we had a real shot at getting on the air.

Once Billy was on board, it was clear the show was going to pilot. Since I didn't have any experience making a TV show, CBS surrounded me with talented people who knew how to make one, including show runner Carol Mendelsohn, a veteran of *Melrose Place*. The inner circle was rounded out with Ann Donahue, an A-level writer brought on to help executive-produce, and Danny Cannon, our director.

At the same time, Marg Helgenberger signed up to star as Catherine Willows, a single mother and former showgirl who works the night shift as Grissom's number two. She was beautiful and sexy, and people loved her from *China Beach*. Next, Gary Dourdan was hired to play Warrick Brown, a recovering gambling addict who's now an investigator. He was one of three actors up for the part, and after his final audition several CBS executives turned to me and asked for my opinion. I didn't have any experience casting actors, but I knew better than to fake it. I picked Gary.

The others concurred. George Eads was hired the day before we shot the pilot. His Texas drawl and humble nature made him a perfect Nick Stokes, a young CSI who came to Vegas from the Dallas crime lab. At each stage, from casting to writing log lines for the first six shows, I learned as much as possible about the process. I paid attention to everything. I asked questions and took notes. I felt like I was back in school.

Everyone understood I was the new kid on the block, but not a single person condescended or took advantage.

Some showed me the way, and others let me learn on my own. As we made the pilot, they were, to one degree or another, doing the same thing themselves. We all had to figure out how to work with each other as much as we had to figure out *CSI.*

Soon it was time for the upfronts, the annual spring gathering when network executives head to New York to present their fall schedules, introduce their new shows, and launch advertising sales. That spring, CBS was hyping two new series, *The Fugitive* and *Survivor. CSI* was the last pitch they bought, the last pilot they green-lit, and the last pilot ordered to series. We barely had time to pack for New York. We didn't care. We were on the schedule.

At the last minute, though, another production re-quiring my immediate attention forced me to drop out of the upfronts trip. Jennifer's water broke the day before I was scheduled to leave, triggering a long, difficult labor, which was further complicated when the doctor saw the umbilical cord was wrapped around the baby's neck. Her doctor ordered an emergency C-section and then, as he worked, asked, "Anthony, are you ready to see your baby?"

In a matter of seconds, the doctor pulled the baby out, snipped the cord, and handed it to the nurse. All through Jennifer's pregnancy, I had talked to her belly, having been told the baby could hear my voice, and sure enough, as the nurse swaddled him in a blanket, I said, "Dawson."

In that moment, I swear time stopped, and I saw my-self—a guy who had been rejected by his father, who him-self had been given up for adoption—with a chance to do better. When time started again, it was because this baby who was about forty-five seconds old turned and looked at me, with wide, alert eyes. He knew my voice.

"Welcome to this wonderful world," I said, crying. "I love you."

The next day *CSI* was formally put on CBS's prime-time schedule for the fall of 2000. Carol and Ann called from the party in New York.

"Congratulations," Carol said. "In your case, double congratulations."

"Now comes the fun," Ann chimed in.

"Yeah, the work," Carol said, laughing.

Work was about to start, and I had a big problem. Jennifer was unhappy about being left in Las Vegas with a new baby, in a house we had just bought, while I went to LA. But there didn't seem to be a choice. The hours it took to launch a TV series were such that I had to move there. (Nina Tassler had warned it would be harder than anything I'd ever done.) Carol and Ann were already set up in a Burbank office building, and *CSI* was set to shoot in Valencia, about an hour north of Hollywood.

I didn't want to ruin my marriage, but I didn't want to blow my chance to play a significant role in the show, either. So I had to make a choice. Did I want to be a technical consultant, receive a small fee, and lose my voice at the writers' table? Or did I want to be fully involved?

I wasn't the first Type-A person in television who had faced this dilemma. Carol offered to set up a schedule where I could come to the set a few days a week and work remotely the rest of the week. If I took advantage of that thoughtful offer, I wouldn't be involved in the daily production issues. Essentially, I'd be an outsider on my own show. No, I had to be involved, *very* involved.

I talked it out with Jennifer. This was my shot, I said. If I was going to be in the business, build a reputation, and make any money, I couldn't just be *associated* with the show. I had to be there, physically present, at all hours, with sleeves rolled up, getting dirty.

Jennifer wasn't happy, but she understood. After all, my mom had just quit her job at the Tropicana after seventeen years for the opposite reason—she wanted to spend time with her first grandchild.

I never doubted my decision. Once work started, I lived and breathed *CSI*. Work began at seven or eight in the morning and went till 9 p.m., often later. It wasn't unusual to look up from lunch and see that it was dark outside. When production began, the hours stretched even longer, from 5 a.m. until midnight or later. No one punched a clock.

For me, the first few weeks of *CSI* were a crash course in TV production. I watched Carol put together a team of writers and studied Ann as she broke down the pilot episode, making sure everything worked. Standing at the whiteboard, she wrote the details down like a math professor. The unit was introduced through the eyes of a new CSI named Holly on her first day of work. There were two other subplots, nine flashbacks, seven close-ups on the science, and more. Grissom's case was in the Act Three tease.

I had written the pilot, and I had no idea it broke down like that until I saw Ann diagram it. Once it was laid out, we began tinkering, adding little details, moving pieces around. Despite the changes, Carol and Ann honored the procedural structure and stylistic choices I had made on the page. In fact, they improved it, digging deeper into those elements. As a result, *CSI* debuted with a fully formed vision and voice.

My biggest challenge was keeping up. I was assigned to write the second episode. That script, despite being a continuation of the pilot, took three times longer to write. It was like coming up with a second album after a multi-platinum debut. I felt serious *pressure*. I wanted to impress Carol and Ann, as well as the network, and I knew respect didn't come overnight—it had to be earned. For a writer, the only way is to deliver the goods.

Ann tackled the third episode, "Crate 'n Burial." Writing scripts can be a lot like constructing elaborate figure eights—you need lots of twists. They're puzzles within puzzles, with similar features each episode. If you don't have the knack for constructing the questions, and then figuring out the answers, forget it. You can learn how to do it better, but you need to start with the gift, and both Carol and Ann had a facility that was as intimidating as it was inspiring.

I realized that I wasn't going to outwrite anyone on this show. Nor was I going to outproduce them. My ideas were good, but so were other people's. And everyone worked hard. We were competing for viewers, competing against other shows, competing against the lowered expectations the network had for us compared with *The Fugitive*, and most of all we were competing against ourselves. We aimed for greatness—whatever that meant.

For the *CSI: Crime Scene Investigation* premiere, on

Friday night, October 6, 2000, Jennifer flew into town and we got a room at the Beverly Hills Hotel. She had put up with my insane hours, and, with her history at the hotel, I wanted to treat her to the softer side of the stairs. We ordered strawberries and champagne from room service, and CBS sent chocolates and flowers. It was a perfect evening, and without the stress of wondering whether the show was good.

We had already seen the first episode. About two months earlier, director Danny Cannon had shown me an early cut. I was too close to the material and couldn't tell if it was any good. I knew it wasn't *bad*. But it was different from what I had seen in my head when I wrote it. Jennifer watched it separately and swore it was "really good." Then the TV critic for the *St. Louis Post-Dispatch* called the episode "a mess" and added, "If *CSI* doesn't shape up and scale down, it could become the first corpse of the new season."

By the time the episode aired, my opinion didn't matter. Neither did the critics'. The only question was what the public would think. Would they watch? Would enough of them watch?

A few hours after the show aired, I called a special hotline to get the ratings—the fast nationals, as they were called. I wrote down the numbers: *CSI* had scored a 14.1/22 share. I wasn't an expert, but when I compared those figures to all the other shows that night, and that week, they looked pretty good to me. In fact, they looked better than pretty good.

"I think we might have won the week," I told Jennifer. "We killed *The Fugitive*. From what I can tell, we beat almost everyone."

Then the phone rang. Apparently everyone else had checked the fast nationals, too. Calls came in from Les, Nina, Billy, Cindy, Carol, Ann, and Marg. *CSI* had finished the week in seventh place.

Two weeks later, Phil Rosenthal, the TV critic for the *Chicago Sun-Times*, captured the rocket ride that was beginning when he wrote, "As far as ratings go, *CSI* is spelled W-O-W." As he and others noted, it was "the surprise of the season."

I read every article just to confirm that what was happening was real. In TV, you don't often have the luxury of finding yourself. Ratings are either good or you're toast, as was the case that fall with new shows from Michael Richards, Bette Midler, and John Goodman. But *CSI*'s numbers held.

"Obscured by the hype for the much higher-profile shows this season, including two others on the same network (*Bette* and *The Fugitive*), *CSI* has emerged as a series that viewers go out of their way to see," the *New York Times* declared. "The series grabbed viewers in its first week on the air in October and has only gotten stronger."

Indeed, *CSI* was among the top ten shows in each of the first four weeks. We were a hit.

There wasn't time to celebrate, though. We were too busy—and too exhausted. The entire cast and crew worked long hours, with the writing staff often staying the longest. To avoid wasting time in traffic, I decided to live in a cheap hotel near the set—it was full of low-wage laborers, transients, hookers, addicts, and the executive producer of TV's hottest new show. On my third night there, when I angled the TV so I could see it from the bed, a crack pipe rolled out from behind.

Fearing I might turn into a real-life CSI case, I moved into another nearby motel, this one a step up in that it offered cable TV. A week or two later, I moved again after returning from my weekend in Vegas and finding a No Vacancy sign in front of the hotel.

After work one night, I tried to check into yet another motel—late-night check-ins weren't out of the ordinary for these places—but my credit card was declined and I didn't have any cash. I drove back to the set and slept in my car. Working in TV definitely was not glamorous.

One day Carol noticed dark circles under my eyes. She warned that the season was a marathon, not a sprint. Agreed.

But no matter how tired, sick, or brain-dead I was, I looked forward to walking into the writers' room every day. It was the show's nerve center. Carol ran it like a think tank. She focused on one episode at a time, breaking down each act, asking questions about each character and each storyline, examining the logic, and double-checking the accuracy. Each session began with the same inquiry: "What is this episode about?"

We worked deep into the minutiae. Who are we following? What are they doing? Why is this action or that detail important? What are the clues? What is the science? Does it work? The questions were endless.

We outlined each episode on the whiteboard: first the opening, then act one, then the middle of act two, and so on. We stared at the board until our eyes blurred, and we paged through our bible, *Practical Homicide Investigation*. Writer and coproducer Josh Berman was particularly fond of reading murder reports in the *Los Angeles Times* and bringing up bizarre killings he would read about online— say, a fatal dog attack blamed on the victim's pheromone-based cosmetics.

"People would've thought we were smoking dope in here," Josh told *Entertainment Weekly*. When we got stuck, we took a walk, broke for lunch, tossed plastic toys at each other, and stared back at the board.

One of my fondest memories of the writers' room came during the first week. Carol was breaking down the structure of the show when she pointed to one of the flashbacks I had written into the pilot and said, "Normally when a writer uses a flashback or re-creation, it's a crutch and we don't allow it. But the way you've done it here modernizes a traditional format. It freshens the storytelling. We want to honor that." Later, Ann quipped, "Thank God you didn't know what you were doing."

From then on, I knew Carol and Ann were both brilliant at structuring a script, and weren't afraid to break the rules. As Billy Petersen later noted, they figured out how to shoot fingerprints and hair follicles. They made the visuals as exciting as the drama. They had to—they had to do it all—if they wanted to achieve Carol's goal of reinventing the TV procedural drama.

The three of us grew close very quickly. You spend so much time together sharing ideas, writing, editing, and rewriting each other that the chemistry either works or it doesn't. In our case, it did. We went through a similar process with the rest of the staff. At the same time everyone was getting to know each other, they were also learning about the characters, figuring out where they came from, what they were all about, and how they interacted.

Thanks to my original research and Carol's and Ann's experience, we had a good handle on *CSI*'s characters before the first show aired; we got even better after half a dozen shows. We had been talking about and living with Grissom, Catherine, and the others as if they were real people. We talked about them at lunch, at dinner; when I called home, I told my wife what we had them do that day; I went to bed and woke up thinking about them.

The lines were definitely blurred. One day we were debating a point in a script and I had Eli Talbert, one of the writers, get on the floor. I grabbed his ankles and dragged him across the carpet in front of Carol and Ann. I wanted to show them that the clasp on his watch would pick up fibers from the carpet.

"It's Locard's Exchange Theory," I said, referring to Edmond Locard, who ran the first crime lab in France in the early 1900s. "Pretend this room is a motel. If he was killed here, but then his body was dragged outside and dumped in a remote desert location, his watch might contain carpet fibers that could be traced back to this particular motel where the crime took place."

Some folks were pretty upset when CBS moved the show to Thursday night at 9 p.m., after *Survivor*. I was among the few who supported the network's decision. It wasn't that I rolled over and agreed to anything. Sure, I was naïve when it came to television, but I was also competitive. In terms of TV viewing, Thursday was the biggest night of the week. We were going up against NBC's "Must-See TV." If *CSI* was as good as I thought, we'd hold our audience and maybe even gain new viewers. To me, it was like playing in the Super Bowl. I wanted to be there. I was eager to see how we'd do.

As it turned out, we did even better on Thursdays. In April 2001, TV critics called CBS's Thursday night lineup "powerful," noting that NBC's domination of the night was being threatened for the first time in two decades. The next month, CBS picked us up for a second season— and sent presents. It was fantastic.

We finished the season with a strong script ("Strip Strangler") from Ann and a party at Billy Petersen's house. As people sipped champagne and nibbled steak and seafood, Billy poured me a scotch and took me outside so we could have a private moment. With just the two of us on his front porch, he lifted his glass.

"Here's to you," he said. "When we first met, I didn't even know you could write. After you pitched me, I was in. You created something great."

The fact was and will always be, Billy Petersen had as

much to do with *CSI*'s success as anyone. I knew the value he had brought to the show, and it meant a lot to hear him pay back the compliment. Later that night and all the next day as I drove back to Vegas, I could only think, Wow, what a ride. What an amazing, unbelievable ride. A few years earlier, I was the assistant garbanzo bean in the ad department at the Mirage. Now I was married, a father, and the creator of TV's number two drama—behind *ER*.

Wow.

47

Jennifer and I moved into a new home in Las Vegas's West Valley, which she decorated with plush furniture and rich, warm colors—except for my lair in the back of the house. A small room, it was a disaster of clashing colors and furniture, tinged with the aroma of cigar smoke, and any interior designer worth their chintz would have cordoned it off with yellow police tape. Then again, in a way, that police tape was what paid for the house.

Living nearby was *CSI's* biggest fan—my mom, who was between jobs. One day I was watching her feed Dawson lunch when I noticed her fingers were gnarled and swollen. Self-conscious, she hid her hands under the table.

"What?" she asked.

"Even from me?" I said.

"What are you talking about?"

"Your hands," I said. "Your fingers are bent and—"

She lifted her right hand, looked at it, and then fed Dawson another spoonful of SpaghettiOs.

"Arthritis," she said. "That's what happens when you deal cards for eighteen years."

I didn't know what to say. It was one of the few times

in my life when I was speechless. My silence, though, wasn't from a lack of caring. No, the sight of those misshapen, painful hands released a flow of emotions and memories that overwhelmed me. Much of the opportunity I had to indulge my creativity and believe in myself was due to my mom. It had been her encouragement and the sacrifices she had made that provided me with a good education and the chance to be a success. I should have said thank you on the spot but I didn't—only because I was unable to say anything. However, as my dad might have said, I filed it away.

"Speaking of work," she said, "I heard from Eddie a couple of weeks ago. He's working at LensCrafters."

"At the mall?" I asked.

She nodded, with a slight wince.

I had the same thought. I had a hard time picturing my dad working in the mall. How did he end up in there? What did he look like? Had he asked my mom about me? I kept those questions to myself. I didn't want to reopen old wounds. After all, I'd turned the page on that relationship—or so I thought.

Eddie in the mall.

I kept trying to picture him taking care of people in LensCrafters.

I tried to picture him, period.

I wondered if he knew about *CSI*. The local papers had done stories about me before last Christmas and I had been mentioned in a few other features on the show. It was likely he knew. Surely one of his friends had shown him the *Las Vegas Sun* or *USA Today* and said, "Isn't that your kid?" I would've loved to have heard his response, but then I'd accepted our lack of a relationship long ago for what it was.

As Grissom might have said, "The facts told the story."

48

In early 2002, a third of the way through *CSI*'s second season, I was among a group of *CSI* executive produc- ers that included Jerry Bruckheimer, Jonathan, Carol, and Ann, who were summoned to CBS for a meeting with the network's top executives, including Leslie Moonves and Nina Tassler, the two who had played such an instrumen- tal role in putting the show on the air.

As we gathered in the executive-floor conference room, we assumed the meeting was good news. In TV, you never knew. But the mood was upbeat. *CSI* was now TV's top-rated drama, and Jerry was also contributing to the network's success with his reality series, *The Amazing Race*. Between the two, he was responsible for big ratings across a wide demographic.

First, we engaged in a general discussion about *CSI*, including favorite episodes, why the show had worked, and where it was headed. Someone brought up a comment I'd made in *Entertainment Weekly* about the show having evolved in season one to a place where most shows were in their third season. At the time of the interview, I had been holding a book on primate anatomy, research for an episode that involved a gorilla attack.

I caught Nina smiling. Leslie had just said something to her. Then he gave all of us an assignment.

"Pick a city," he said.

I didn't understand.

"Pick a city."

Jerry immediately spoke up and said Miami. And with that *CSI: Miami* was created.

The network was excited, the word *franchise* was used for the first time, and the three of us who spent our lives in the writers' room took the order as the ultimate compliment.

At the same time, it was the ultimate challenge. We were expected to maintain the quality and strength of *CSI* while creating a second show that would be a disaster if it was anything less than a hit. Outside, I stood in the parking lot with Carol and Ann.

"No pressure, right?" I said.

"I'm going back to LA," Carol said. "I have a show to run."

Ann, who had been pegged to run the new show, turned to me.

"I guess we're going to Miami tomorrow," she said.

We had a ton of research to do, and time was of the essence since we were introducing the new show with a crossover episode in the middle of *CSI*'s season.

"At least we can sleep on the plane," I said.

Once in Miami, we toured South Beach, Little Havana, downtown, midtown, Little Haiti, and other neighborhoods. In Little Havana, we stopped for pressed sandwiches and watched older Cuban men play chess and smoke cigars. We took notes and talked about locations in and around LA that looked like Miami.

On the second day, we rode around with Dade County investigators, just as I had done with the Las Vegas Police Department. One of the first calls we went on was to a run-down two-bedroom home where investigators were dealing with a dead body.

The owner had been a hoarder. He had filled every square inch of the place with boxes and junk, leaving only narrow pathways from room to room. I knew it was going to be gruesome when we smelled the stench of his rotting corpse from two blocks away. We were trying not to gag as we walked up to the front, but the cops loved our reaction. They were more relaxed than the Vegas guys. They lit up cigars as we walked up to the house.

"To cut the smell," one officer explained, offering me one.

I lit it and handed it to Ann.

"Just smell it," I said. "You don't have to inhale."

It didn't help. With the smell filling the air like a thick, inescapable cloud, we were reluctant to enter the house, but we bowed to the cops' encouragement and our own curiosity. Inside, we encountered a dead man lying on a queen-size bed. A porn tape was paused midscene on the TV. One officer later explained that it had been on a loop. The dead man was discolored, distorted, and simply enormous—larger than any human being I had ever seen.

"He must be three or four hundred pounds," I said.

"No," one of the investigators said. "He's probably about your size, about one eighty."

"But he's *huge*," I said.

"It's all gaseous fluids," the cop said.

"What happens with *that*?" I asked, then quickly added, "Do I want to know?"

He and another guy nearby shook their heads. With that, Ann and I bolted out the door. As we were trying to drink in some fresh air, a van rolled up and three large men got out wearing white hazardous material suits. One of the guys nodded, thinking I was a cop.

"What's up?" I said.

"Man, we were about to go to the Heat game," he said. "Then we got this call. Heard you have a situation we got to take care of."

The three of them carried tools that looked like long harpoons. They marched in and approached the body. We followed, but backed off to a relatively safe distance after watching them assess the bloated corpse as if it were a dead whale that had beached itself on the sand. One of them poked the body lightly with his harpoon. Then, after giving each other a quick nod, they secured masks over their faces, and one of them said, "Let's do it." With quick, sharp jabs, they lanced the guy's gut, unleashing streams of bloody fluids and even more noxious-smelling fumes. It was a disgusting mess.

But it did the trick. The guy's bloated body deflated by half. He was then wrapped in a hazmat bag and prepped for removal. Another guy with a Mr. T–style Mohawk entered the bedroom holding a giant chain saw. He moved with a business-as-usual calm as he put on goggles, revved up his saw, and cut out a portion of the wall by the window, creating a way to remove the body. I noticed the house was on a slab; the wall came right out. Then a forklift drove into the room, scooped up the body, and carted it out.

Meanwhile, one of the CSIs was looking up repairmen in the Yellow Pages and getting bids on replacing the window. I was sure I had picked up some kind of airborne virus.

"You can't make this stuff up," I said to Ann.

Indeed, after cramming in as much as possible in a few days, including more crime scenes and a visit to the coroner's office, we returned to LA and began to figure out the new show. On the plane, Ann noted the key difference in sensibility: *CSI* was a dark show where the action took place at night; *CSI: Miami* would take place in the daytime. That alone helped us establish a visual sensibility. As I added, "People go to Vegas to escape. They go to Miami to be seen."

Above all, we needed a lead actor for the new show. We were introducing the new series in an episode scheduled for early May. With less than two months before we shot, and the script in the earliest draft, we knew the story's bare bones. Grissom and Willows were going to follow an investigation to Miami and hook up with their South Florida counterpart, Lieutenant Horatio Caine. So who could play Caine?

Billy Petersen had shown us the importance of having a powerful actor in the driver's seat. We wanted someone just as forceful, but different. From the beginning, the network liked David Caruso. When I first heard his name, I said no. I had heard he was difficult to work with, but people looked at me like the rookie I was. It was a classic misjudgment on my part. Other names were tossed around for a nanosecond, but David was the guy everyone liked. He even lived in Miami.

David flew in and met Carol, Ann, and me for a steak dinner in Beverly Hills. I immediately understood why the network thought he was perfect for the role. He was a leading man. Heads turned as he entered the restaurant wearing blue jeans, a white T-shirt, and a leather jacket; you could feel the change in the room. He had charisma, the kind of juice an actor must have to command an audience, and he had it without trying.

We could see he wasn't interested in the star trip that some have when they walk into a restaurant, wondering who's there and who's noticed them; in David's case, he was comfortable with himself, focused on us, and didn't waste any time getting to the point. As soon as we sat down, he threw all of his cards on the table. He wanted the job. He said that people still saw him as his *NYPD Blue* character, Detective John Kelly. Since 9/11, he'd been repeatedly stopped on the street and asked how he was going to fix things.

"What do I know about that?" he said. "I'm an actor."

One with a history. But I liked that David didn't

bother dispelling any stories we might have heard about him; they didn't interest him. Whatever had happened in the past, true or false, was in the past, which was a great way to be. Instead, David talked about being a passionate actor who was married to his work, and the personal growth he had made since his earlier roles. He spoke about his philosophy of life, death, and crime, and the show we had already created; amazingly enough, but not surprisingly, for David life, death, and acting were all connected.

Before the bread was on the table, he was comparing making great television to practicing a religion. By the time our salads arrived, Carol and Ann kicked me under the table and whispered, "He's the one. He's our guy."

After dinner, we welcomed David onto the show. We knew the network executives already liked him. Later, I heard that someone at the network took him aside and said, "We're giving you the crown jewels. Don't screw it up."

Now we just had to make sure we didn't.

49

David understood his role and was never anything less than a star. I channeled a lot of his personal energy as I worked on his character, a cop whose obsession with integrity is his way of dealing with the constant pain he bears from personal tragedy. He was the opposite of the constrained Grissom. All emotion, Caine was a frayed nerve bristling in the open air.

We introduced *CSI: Miami* in the *CSI* episode titled "Cross Jurisdiction," which had Grissom and Willows heading to Miami as they investigated the death of a former Vegas chief of detectives whose wife and daughter were also missing. A month later, CBS announced *CSI: Miami* was going to be part of its fall lineup in 2002. In July, we faced the press at the annual Television Critics Association event in Pasadena.

I was asked about doing a spin-off so soon. "Is it scary?" I asked, repeating the question. "Absolutely."

David shared his excitement. "Just to get to go for a ride on this concept is ideal for an actor," he said. His return to TV was big news, as was the show itself, which a writer for the New York *Daily News* called "the closest thing to a surefire hit among the new fall shows."

As I frequently said, "No pressure."

Ann and I shared writing duties on the pilot, "Golden Parachute." David's cool persona helped me envision Caine's first scene: standing amid the wreckage of an airplane in a swampy area, surveying the crash scene and coming upon young cop Eric Delko pounding on a victim's chest, trying to revive him.

"I lost him," Delko says.

"It happens," Caine tells him.

"He could've told us something."

"We don't need him to," Caine says, taking in the debris. "We've got the whole story right here."

Boom—we were into the first show, which was built around a case involving a private jet crash in the Everglades. One woman's body was five miles from the crash site, and one survivor told a story that didn't make sense. It was classic *CSI*—let the facts lead you to the solution. However, we didn't have a finished draft when we arrived in Miami, where we had twelve days to shoot the pilot, and complicating matters even further, we had a problem with act four—it didn't work.

We weren't able to tie the show together. It was what happened when you didn't spend weeks with a staff dissecting every element. As Ann and I reminded ourselves, though, we didn't have time to be blocked. We couldn't shoot until we had solved the script problem.

For several days, the two of us holed up in the Loews hotel in Miami Beach, drank massive amounts of coffee, and shared rewrites. We talked on the phone, emailed notes, and yelled to each other from our balconies. In the middle of our second day of nonstop work, I looked at myself in the mirror—unshaven, my eyes red, wearing a hotel bathrobe and my underwear, basically a loser writer locked on the twenty-third floor of a hotel overlooking a beach full of hot women in bikinis—and I burst into deranged laughter.

I realized that despite all the stress, I loved the challenge of having to write myself out of this mess. I was Houdini in shackles, locked in a safe and lowered into a pool of water, and I had to get out before I drowned. Even though the job had its dangers and difficulties, and might destroy me, I wouldn't have traded places with anyone. I was a maniac.

At the end of the second day, following nearly forty-eight hours of sleepless work fueled by M&Ms and chips from the minibar, Ann and I worked out the problems, connected the dots between act one and act four, and finally typed "The End."

"We got it!" I yelled into the phone. "We figured it out!"

A second later, Ann ran out onto her balcony and screamed, "We did it! And it's better than sex!"

50

We shot the opening scene in the Everglades, the site of our plane crash. Ann and I watched on monitors as a police helicopter flew low over the ground and David Caruso sauntered across the field, looking at scattered debris from the wreckage. As cameras rolled, a wild boar ran into the scene. Someone else spotted an alligator. I gave Ann a gentle nudge.

"We're doing it again, aren't we?" I said. "We're actually doing this."

"Yeah," she said. "We are."

"Unbelievable."

On the third day of shooting, David asked me if he could wear sunglasses on camera. We were doing a lot of exteriors, and he said the sun was bothering him. I didn't think it was a good idea. I wanted to see his eyes. But I didn't want him to be uncomfortable, so I said, "Sure, no problem."

Of course, once Caruso put the glasses on, we couldn't get them off. They became part of his character, and I sensed he had wanted that all along. When *CSI: Miami* debuted on September 23, 2002, the show drew 23 million viewers, rocketing it straight into TV's top five series. "Fans can relax; the franchise is in good, and possibly even better, hands," wrote *USA Today*. Speaking to Paula Zahn on CNN, David explained the spirit all of us felt behind the scenes. "The assemblage of people, and being a part of the *CSI* family, was so effortless for all of us, it would be great if we could do the show for a while."

Later, David spoke to *USA Today* about the show "fitting into an existing format that is already working" and how "there's a lot of relief in that. There's a lot of inherent trust in what is going on." But not everyone was as happy with *CSI: Miami*. Billy Petersen wasn't a fan of the spin-off. As both star and executive producer, he thought the network was devaluing the original and wished they had waited a few more seasons before creating another *CSI*. "It's everything we can do to get our show done," he told *Chicago Sun-Times* TV writer Phil Rosenthal. "If our show starts to suffer, I'll go berserk."

I understood, and I would have also come unglued if *Miami* had cannibalized the original's quality or ratings. But I understood CBS's position. With imitations popping up on every network (*Crossing Jordan*, *Dragnet*, *John Doe*, and even *Without a Trace* on CBS), expanding the *CSI* franchise was also a way of protecting it, as long as we maintained the exceptionally high standards we had created for ourselves and the audience.

And we did. By spring 2003, *CSI: Miami* was in the top ten (or just below it), and *CSI*, in addition to being TV's number one or two series, was broadcast in 175 countries, making it the most-watched program in the world. In May, I received an honorary doctorate of humane letters from my alma mater, UNLV. I had tears in my eyes during the ceremony. Along with winning an Oscar and an Emmy, getting a doctorate was one of my dreams. Dr. Zuiker—I loved the way it sounded.

I also loved the challenge Leslie Moonves presented a few months later. It was early 2004, and the CBS chief was hosting a dinner to celebrate *CSI: Miami*'s renewal. Midway through the meal, he made a toast and then, after a mischievous smile, he said, "Pick a city."

We had already known a third *CSI* was on the drawing board—he'd admitted that to the press the previous fall. But now that it was a reality, you could hear the collective *uh-oh* from those of us at the table.

As for picking a city, I immediately thought of Washington, DC. In the aftermath of 9/11, it seemed a ripe setting for another show, and I blurted out "Quantico." No one liked it. I tried again, this time saying, "New York." It won instant approval. Within the week, we had laid the groundwork for introducing the new show at the end of *CSI: Miami*'s second season, and Carol and I began planning a trip to New York.

Despite all my success, security, and recognition in the press, a part of me still wasn't satisfied. In an interview with the *New York Times*, I might have exposed too much of my psychopathology when I admitted, "What I'm trying to do is get somebody to say: 'That kid is a true talent. That kid's got vision. That kid's an animal. Kid loves to compete, loves to write, loves to create.'"

But who exactly was that person I wanted to hear it

from? I didn't need a therapist to figure it out—I had a wife. Before leaving for New York, I went home to Vegas and Jennifer suggested looking up my father. She wondered if telling him about *CSI* might help to relieve some of the pain I carried from the past and calm the insatiable need I had to prove myself.

"How long has it been since you've talked to him?" she asked.

"A couple of years ago at the casino," I told her.

"No, I mean *really* talked to him."

I scratched my head.

"I wrote him a letter when I was sixteen," I said. "I fired him as my father."

"And that followed a positive experience, didn't it?" she asked sarcastically.

I shuddered.

"Maybe you should call him," she said.

Through my mom, I knew Eddie's life had spiraled depressingly downward, but I didn't know to what degree. Nor did I know he was trying to negotiate a move to Florida from Las Vegas. He had bought some land there, had mapped out a route, and wanted to buy a mobile home. Money was tight, though, and time was running out.

Even though I knew Jennifer was right, I wasn't ready or interested in opening that door again, so I didn't contact Eddie. Interestingly enough, I went to Caesars Palace for lunch and to place a few bets at the sports book, and instead found myself wandering through a gift shop at the mall. There, I bought a large ceramic egg-shaped jar called a Wish Pot. I had no idea why it caught my attention, though I was intrigued once I learned its purpose.

The top had a long string connected to it on the inside. You were supposed to write a wish on a piece of paper, clip it to the end of the string, put the lid back on, and let the wish brew. When your wish came true, you were supposed to give the pot to someone else.

I intended to give it to Jennifer, but forgot it in the back of my car and took it with me to Los Angeles. Maybe that was the plan all along. The Wish Pot ended up in my hotel suite, and a day or two later, I removed it from its box and placed it on a shelf between the bar area and the door. But first, I wrote a wish and clipped it to the string:

"I wish I could find forgiveness for my father."

51

Soon after, Carol and I traveled to New York to prepare for the new series. As we did our research, we saw that the city's wounds from the 9/11 attack two years earlier were still raw, and the stories we heard were more emotional than in either Vegas or Miami. Take the medical examiner we spoke to at the coroner's office. He told us how he had coped with all the bodies brought in after the planes flew into the Twin Towers.

"Except they weren't bodies," he explained. "They were body *parts*."

He showed us the makeshift tents outside that had been used for processing. They were still working on cases, he said. He walked us into a chapel that was full of cards, letters, and photos of people who had died. He also introduced us to a man who was still sorting through the human remains, trying to use DNA to determine identities.

Then he took us into a refrigerated room where we saw row after row of silver packets, each one stenciled with a name and an American flag. They held little pieces of the 9/11 victims—an arm, a toe, an eyeball. The coroner mentioned that they had actually isolated the remains of Mohammed Atta, the lead terrorist who had flown the first American Airlines jet into the World Trade Center.

"They'll be destroyed and dumped at sea so no place on US soil will become a shrine to his martyrdom," he said.

Before leaving, I noticed a quote from Pope John Paul II pinned on the examiner's office bulletin board: "A society will be judged on the basis of how it treats its weakest members, and among the most vulnerable are surely the unborn and the dying." It was the kind of emotional detail needed to help envision the new series.

With Carol running *CSI* and Ann heading up *CSI: Miami*, CBS put me in charge of *CSI: NY*. It was an enormous vote of confidence, considering I was only four years into this business. But I felt ready. It helped when award-winning actor Gary Sinise accepted the lead role of Detective Mac Taylor. In early 2004, we had met at a Mexican restaurant near his LA home. I walked in wearing a new three-piece suit. He came dressed in a T-shirt, shorts, and flip-flops. I looked like his attorney.

Nevertheless, we hit it off. I pitched him the show, which I envisioned as more character-driven than the two other *CSI* series, which focused on procedure. I explained how the stories I had heard in New York had influenced my take on the show and how I wanted to provide an outlet for the cops I'd met there. They had so much to say, and for a writer, it was profoundly rich material.

Gary agreed. Within thirty minutes, he was speaking as if Mac Taylor already existed. Great actors slip into a role and then expand it, literally and, in his case, creatively. There, at the table, we began working up relationships with other characters. In the middle of one riff, he stopped and said, "Boy, it would be great to work together."

"I think we already are," I said.

Next, I met with Melina Kanakaredes for the role of Stella Bonasera, Taylor's second-in-command. She was an Emmy-nominated actress who had starred in movies and spent five years on the hit series *Providence*. In other words, like Gary, she was another pro. When we met for lunch in Laguna Beach, I was impressed that she was even smarter and more beautiful in person. Then we added Carmine Giovinazzo, Eddie Cahill, Hill Harper, Vanessa Ferlito, and the rest of the cast.

On May 17, 2004, *CSI: NY* was introduced in an episode of *CSI: Miami* titled "MIA/NYC Nonstop," where the clue to a double homicide took David Caruso's Caine to New York and he encounters Mac Taylor. The big news was that the spin-off was scheduled to go head-to-head with NBC's *Law & Order* franchise. The best news? The crossover episode was another ratings hit.

I wrapped my arms around all that encouragement as I slipped away to write the pilot episode. It came out aggressive, bleak, and emotional—the way I had always envisioned it. Detective Taylor was an ex-Marine turned cop who had lost his wife on 9/11. He kept a pile of unsolved cases on his desk, a constant reminder of both the work to be done and his own lingering pain.

One of my favorite moments of that first episode came halfway into the story when Taylor and Stella Bonasera find a comatose woman in the basement of a Queens home and take her to the hospital. As Taylor sits next to her bed, he spills his guts for what seems like the first time.

"I'm tired," he says. "I used to sit like this with my wife. Her name was Claire. She died on 9/11. Nobody saw it coming. I was cleaning out the closet the other day, and I—I found this beach ball. And I remembered it was my wife who blew it up. I never told anybody this, but I got rid of everything that reminded me of Claire. Too painful. The one thing I couldn't throw away was that beach ball. Her breath is still in there."

To me, that scene, and the pilot as a whole, was one of my best pieces of writing ever. I was incredibly proud of it. After the network handed back notes, which weren't extensive, director Deran Sarafian shot the hell out of the script, and we premiered it for CBS executives and advertisers in New York. It aired on September 22, 2004, and drew about 18 million viewers, numbers that indicated another hit.

But I didn't hear the sound of champagne corks being popped. The next morning, as I drove down Sunset Boulevard, one of the network's top programming executives called, concerned that the show was too dark, too depressing, and too unlike *CSI*. He wasn't alone. The Associated Press had described the series opener as having "a dour mood."

"While *CSI: NY* resembles its fellow forensics dramas in the sort of crimes it tackles, the need to set this edition apart from the others has resulted in dusky visuals and laconic dialogue that make the show as deadly as its subject matter," the AP critic said. "There's no flashy Vegas decadence or Sunshine State glow to play the crime against. Just grinding urban despair."

I had trouble understanding the critique because the numbers were excellent. Only a few shows on the air wouldn't have wanted that kind of audience share. A meeting with several key executives at CBS, including Leslie and Nina, helped enlighten me. While understanding where I had come from as a writer, and even praising the validity of the characters, they talked about the relationship viewers had to the franchise itself, their expectations, and the potential for damaging that if we were to take *CSI: NY* in such a severe direction.

"I know how these things go," Leslie said. "You start at fourteen million, then the ratings slip to ten, then seven, and then the next thing it's off the air. You have to make some fixes."

Although I was tense during the meeting and in knots afterward as I wrestled with a sense of having failed, the advice was immensely helpful—and correct. I had forgotten one of the cardinal rules of TV: You have to entertain people. You might be able to challenge your audience with difficult material one week. But probably not a second week. And definitely not a third or fourth.

Before the show got into trouble, I asked Leslie and Nina for help. It turned out to be one of the best moves of my career and something I advise others to heed: Don't be afraid to ask for assistance. They brought in veteran executive producer Pam Veasey, and together we got the show where it needed to be. We showed more of the city's hues, voices, and neighborhoods, as Nina and Leslie had urged.

As I told people, the show wasn't going to avoid dark realities. But we had to earn the right to go there.

Rarely in TV history has an audience waited on the sidelines for the producers to fix a show, but the *CSI: NY* audience understood and gave us time. Over the holidays, we prepped new episodes. Our goal was to turn on the lights. But not all was bleak: *CSI: NY* had been nominated for a People's Choice Award as one of TV's best new dramas. *CSI* also received a nomination as best drama. At the January 9, 2005, ceremony, *CSI* triumphed and all of us involved with *CSI: NY* hoped we would be back again.

Hours later, I was back at my desk, making notes on a script. Later, I wanted to call my mom and tell her about the awards show. I figured she would watch, but I didn't know. That was one of the odd things about making TV. I knew millions of people tuned in every week, but I had no idea who they were. I often wondered if Eddie was among them. But not that morning. I barely looked up from my work when my assistant, Orlin, walked in and put that message slip from Daniel Holstein on the corner of my desk.

PART VIII

CRIME SEEN

52

In February 2005, I received a call from Eddie's professed best friend, Jesse, the one who'd invited me to his place to go through old photos. I'd had Eddie's remains at my place for a few weeks. Jesse said he had been thinking about my old man and felt like reminiscing. He invited me to his place again.

"You sound exactly like your old man," he said.

"Yeah, I've been told," I said.

"I still can't believe Eddie did that to himself," he said. "Every time I think about—"

I cut him off and passed on his invitation. I had given up trying to figure out the details that led to Eddie's putting that sawed-off shotgun in his mouth and pulling the trigger. I'd gone through his papers, knew about his decline, his trip down the employment ladder, and his failed attempt to move to Florida. In a way, that said it all. He was stuck where he was, and he didn't like it. His suicide was his response to the daily agony of disappointment and desperation. He had tried to live life on his own terms, and the best he could do in the end was to leave on his own terms. It wasn't pretty, but I felt like I knew as much as I needed to know—or as much as I was going to get.

I still gave Jesse a moment to talk. He said that he

had an old movie of my dad's that showed me catching a fish. He'd once watched it with Eddie and guessed the old film had been left at his place. He said that Eddie had cared about me. I wish that I'd asked if he'd known about *CSI*, if he'd watched. I didn't think of it. I had turned and stared at the urn holding Eddie's remains. It was next to the ceramic Wish Pot.

"Hey Jesse, what do you think really happened?" I asked. "Was there any one thing upsetting Eddie?"

"You want the truth?" he asked.

"Sure."

"He wasn't getting laid anymore," he said.

After talking with Jesse, who confirmed everything I suspected, I knew it was time to move on. I didn't yet know what I was going to do with Eddie, but I was ready to get back to work. I had plenty waiting for me, too, starting with one of the most exciting episodes in the five-year history of *CSI*. Quentin Tarantino was going to direct the show's fifth-season finale.

Quentin was one of the biggest *CSI* fans I had ever encountered, and when we met at a 9/11 fund-raiser during the show's second season, I gave him a standing invitation to direct an episode. When *CSI*'s tech advisor Larry Mitchell ran into Quentin while shooting in Las Vegas, he floated the idea again, and Quentin set up a meeting with the producers and me, where we offered him the season finale.

It was an unforgettable meeting. Quentin walked in wearing shorts and a T-shirt, flip-flops and a hat. He had an iPod headset dangling under his arm and a large Starbucks cup in his hand. Charming and humble, he looked thrilled to be in *CSI*'s writers' room. While shooting *Kill Bill* in Beijing, he explained, he had watched *CSI* nonstop on his days off, and he knew as much about the show as we did. Grissom, he added, was his favorite TV detective since Columbo.

I wanted to hug him.

But we all were trying to be cool; this was, after all, the Oscar winner responsible for *Reservoir Dogs*, *Pulp Fiction*, *Kill Bill*, and more. As Quentin put his stuff down on the table, he said, "You know, on the way over here I had an idea. Can I tell it to you?"

Within moments, we were spellbound. He began by describing an old cowboy song he had been listening to in the car, some cowpoke campfire tune that none of us knew. And then he connected it to the show, saying, "Wouldn't it be cool if that was a song that Nick's father had played for him as a boy? Because I can see Nick driving along, listening to this old song, which reminds him of a nickname his dad used to call him, Pancho, and we're thinking things are going to be fine. But it isn't. Nothing's ever fine. And it really isn't fine for Nick.

"He doesn't know it, but Nick's going to be kidnapped and put in a box—a clear, plastic box. Not only that, he's going to be buried in that box underneath the ground. He'll be surrounded by explosives, these motion-sensitive explosives, so that if you found him and didn't know better, he'd blow up. But that's not even the worst part.

"Nick's going to have limited air when he's underground. All he's going to have is a light stick and gun with him, so that he can blow his brains out if he goes crazy before he runs out of air. And of course this is all going to be visible via a camera that our villain will have set up so Grissom and the CSIs can watch their colleague die. Unless they pay the million-dollar ransom."

"Perfect dilemma," someone said.

"No, not so perfect," Quentin continued. "That option is going to get messed up when the guy who put him in that situation dies in an explosion. But then Grissom's going to find where Nick is buried by using some great forensic science by tracking these rare kind of fire ants that are eating Nick alive. However, as Grissom digs, Nick's going to see him and freak out. He knows everything's going to blow up if they go any further. But you know what's *really* cool about this?"

At this point, what wasn't?

"So at this moment," Quentin continued, "when they're staring at each other, they have this whole father-son moment that's never really surfaced. It's like the CSI is a surrogate family and Nick has never gotten his due from Grissom, but now, all of a sudden, there's this sense of loss and instantaneous realization of what could be lost . . ."

Quentin paused and looked around the table. I marveled at this guy's genius—he had completely sucked us into his story and got me thinking about my own dad at the same time. Phenomenal! Had Quentin really come up with this idea between Starbucks and the studio? How the eff—

"So," he continued, "I'm thinking that if we did something in that sort of permutation it would be, you know, cool."

Although the meeting was supposed to be exploratory, Quentin, after riffing nonstop for an hour, committed to doing the finale. How could he not? He had pitched a sensational story. Carol, producer Naren Shankar, and I did the heavy lifting on the script, with Quentin adding his own touches, until we were ready to shoot what he called "the *CSI* movie."

Once on the set, Quentin was a force of nature. Good-tempered, open, and focused on getting the best from every moment, he injected new energy in the cast and crew. Not only did it feel like a Tarantino movie, but the set began to look like one when he brought on veteran actor John Saxon and movie legend Tony Curtis. One day, Naren suggested a certain shot, and Quentin turned and said, "Yeah, cool, I did that on *Kill Bill*."

When we shot in Vegas, I stood behind Quentin one day as he shot a scene with Frank Gorshin, the great actor who had played the Riddler on the original *Batman* TV series. Quentin loved working with Gorshin, who died of lung cancer a few days before the episode aired in May. He let Frank, who was a master impressionist and comedian, improvise for about twelve minutes. Quentin yelled "Cut" only when he saw me check my watch. He was annoyed.

"Anthony, I only yelled cut because you're here looking at your watch," Quentin said. "But I have to tell you, I really didn't *want* to yell cut, because this actor standing in front of the camera, Mr. Frank Gorshin, is a genius, and we're privileged to be in his presence. We're privileged to watch him work, as opposed to watching our watches. Don't you think?"

I did.

As Carol said, "Quentin exuded pure joy." But give him a camera and he would shoot until he ran out of film. TV didn't work like that. The show ran sixty minutes— forty-eight minutes without commercials. That one scene with Gorshin was the equivalent of a quarter of the episode. But Quentin ignored the rules. Indulging his passion for story and performance, he really applied movie standards to *CSI*. Pretty soon we were two hours over, with more of the episode left to shoot.

"You know what the solution is?" he said to Carol and me.

No, we didn't.

"It's very simple," Quentin said. "We're doing a two-hour show."

The network agreed. They saw the potential of creating a genuine TV event with a two-parter from Quentin Tarantino. As far as I was concerned, the surest way to make great television was to let great writers put their unique stamp on a show. With Quentin directing, we did exactly that. For me, the father-son aspect of the story gave it a more personal meaning, too. At the wrap party, I gave Quentin a gift from the entire show—my Wish Pot. I could have bought him anything, but at the last minute that struck me as appropriate.

It seemed to confuse Quentin. He picked up the ceramic container, lifted off the top, and stared at the long, noodle-shaped string.

"You're supposed to clip a piece of paper with a wish written on it," I said. "When that comes true, you're supposed to give it to someone else."

"Cool," he said, nodding his head.

Then he noticed a piece of paper clipped near the bottom of the string. It was the wish I'd written.

"Check it out," I said.

Quentin opened it up and smiled.

"Forgiveness," he said.

"Now it's your turn to write down a wish and then pass the pot on after your wish comes true," I said.

53

Goodbyes are said in many ways. Some with waves, some with tears, some with hugs. I wrote mine.

It was the end of 2005, about eight months after the Tarantino episode aired to record-breaking ratings, and I was buried in the new season of *CSI: NY*. After a long day on the set, I returned to my hotel suite to do some more work. I turned on the lights, touched Eddie, and sat down at my desk.

On the agenda: an episode titled "Run Silent, Run Deep," which was a continuation of the story of the Tanglewood Boys, a gang of mobster kids Danny Messer (Carmine Giovinazzo) knew from his old New York days. The original Tanglewood script had ended with one of the guys saying, "Go ask Danny Messer what we do. He knows."

Now, in this second part, the CSIs were going to dig up a body in the end zone at Giants Stadium. They thought it was Jimmy Hoffa. It wasn't. But they were going to find a cigarette, test it for DNA, and it was going to come back a match for Danny Messer. He would then confess to Mac (Gary Sinise) that he was present during the hit, but never said anything, and must have flipped his cigarette into the hole. But he didn't commit the murder.

But in fact the opening teaser was going to reveal one of the Tanglewood Boys, now an adult, in the front seat of his car as he groaned, "I can't do this anymore. I'm totally freaking out. I can't handle it." Then he was going to blow his head off—my homage to Eddie.

With the soundtrack from *Schindler's List* playing in the background, I wrote for hours, thinking about my dad, retracing my steps over the past year, from Daniel Holstein's initial call to the urn where Eddie currently resided near my front door. When I wrote the Tanglewood guy as saying, "I can't do this anymore," I was thinking about my dad and imagining his pain building up, like plaque on the soul. I pictured all those years of regret and guilt—not the criminal kind, but the kind he carried inside for deeds he'd done and mistakes he'd made.

After the trigger was pulled, though, came the release—his and mine. Later, the show's technical advisor told me that the people who put a gun in their mouths never hear the click. It happens too fast. By the time they pull the trigger, they're gone. And so it was with Eddie, and with me, too. With his death, he had released both of us from a painful past that had kept us apart and then brought us together again. Was I wrong to think "gingerbread"?

When we shot the episode, I placed two of Eddie's paintings (one of a shark and one of Jesus) in the opening sequence. Given the quick cuts, it was hard to make them out. But I knew they were there, including one splattered with his blood. For me, it was a fitting farewell.

Soon after finishing that episode, I heard about a friend who was heading to the Caribbean for a two-week sailing vacation. Eddie's final wish was to be buried at sea. I asked my friend if he would take Eddie's ashes and deposit them in the turquoise paradise.

I knew it was a lot to ask and that it might creep him out. But he said sure and asked if I had a particular place in mind.

"Wherever you feel is right," I said.

"All right," he said. "Just bring him over."

A few days later I put Eddie in the car and headed to my friend's house. I didn't make much out of this last father-son ride of ours. By now, everything I had needed to say or do had been said and done. I'd taken care of his bills, cleaned up his place, sorted through his belongings, spoken to his friends, searched for answers to my questions, and ultimately made my peace. When I handed the urn to my friend, it was more bon voyage than goodbye.

Then one day my friend left a message on my cell phone. He said that he'd found an exquisite patch of blue water, tied a bottle of champagne to Eddie's urn, and tossed both overboard. The champagne had been my idea—in case he met a hot mermaid. As far as I was concerned, Eddie and I were good.

The next weekend Jennifer and I took Dawson and Evan, now two years old, to my mom's for dinner. She and David had the day off and had spent it making an Italian feast. He was still a restaurant captain, and my mom was now a pit boss at a small local casino off the Strip called

Terrible's. It was a nice evening. The boys fell asleep as my mom reminisced about watching me work on the *CSI* pilot. She spoke with a dreamy disbelief about being on the set and meeting Billy, Marg, and Gary. I understood. All of us, at different times, had trouble believing such good fortune was real.

"I hoped the show would last a couple weeks," she said.

"Only a couple of weeks?" I said, laughing.

"I didn't know anything about TV," she said. "I wanted you to be happy."

"What about rich?" I asked. "Did you want me to be rich, too?"

That amused her. She had listened to so many of my get-rich-quick schemes as I grew up that one more wasn't going to sway her, not even one as grand as a TV pilot. Besides, she explained, getting rich was not something she thought about, not anything she dreamed about or considered possible. She had survived hard times, and that had made her a hard-core realist. If she'd ever dreamed about getting rich, it had been back when she was with Eddie, and those thoughts had disappeared after he'd left her with a small child.

My mom and I didn't tell many stories about those days. There weren't many pleasant memories compared to the present, which was much better and more exciting. *CSI* had given us a safety net. We didn't have to think about the past, though we couldn't erase it.

Case in point: my mom's arthritic hands. I watched

her rubbing them as she told another story. She noticed me looking at her permanently swollen joints and crooked fingers. I thought about the constant pain those hands gave her. She rarely mentioned the discomfort and complained even less. But suddenly she held them up for me to see and added a what-am-I-going-to-do shrug.

"My feet are worse," she said. "One of the great underreported ailments of our time—standing all day at work."

She couldn't wear high heels anymore.

"In 1978, I was dealing at the Stardust," she told us. "I was a beginner. I had gotten juiced in, and I was working the graveyard. I'll never forget. I was dealing to a guy who was betting a couple hundred dollars a hand, and he had three or four hands going. I kept losing. And the boss came up behind me and said, 'Get the money back.' What was I supposed to do? Then he kicked me in the heel of my shoes. Hard."

"They can't do that," I said.

"*Now* they can't," she said. "But back then they did. I had another boss who slammed his hand down on the podium behind the tables every time I turned over a card and busted. It made me nuts. I was petrified to turn my hand over."

All of a sudden her eyes filled with tears. She got out a tissue and apologized for crying.

"It's just that you've been the most important thing in my life," she said. "More important than anyone—my parents, my husband, anyone. There were many years when

I was struggling, really struggling with things, and Anthony, if not for you, I don't know if I could've gone on."

The following Sunday my mom came to our house before starting her shift at work. She made breakfast for Dawson, Jennifer, and me, and held Evan. She was all about getting in her grandma time. I did the dishes and watched her with the boys.

"What time is your shift?" I asked.

"Eleven," she said.

She checked her watch.

"Oops. That's in twenty minutes. Where'd the time go?"

After she left, I sat in the kitchen and watched Jennifer with the boys. I thought about the different kind of childhoods Dawson and Evan were going to have compared with mine. When I was Dawson's age, my mom worked all night and barely made the rent each month. Sometimes she didn't make it. I shuddered as I remembered being locked out of our apartment right before Christmas and my mom pleading with the landlord to let us back in. Life was different now. She hadn't wanted to leave her grandchildren and go to work, and the thing I realized was that she didn't have to work anymore. Not if she didn't want to—and it was a pretty sure bet she would've preferred to rock a baby on her lap than deal cards for eight hours at Terrible's.

At lunch, I told Jennifer that I had an idea. I'd probably said that to her ten thousand times since we'd been together: *I have an idea.* But look where it had gotten us.

"Yeah?" she said.

"It's a little crazy," I warned.

Then I told her the idea and afterward she wrapped her arms around me.

"It's not crazy," she said. "I actually think it might be the best idea you've had in a long time."

Two and a half hours later, Jennifer and I walked into Terrible's and made our way across the casino. My mom was focused on the four people playing blackjack at her table and didn't see us approaching. When she did glance up from her deal, she gave me a puzzled look. At first, she was concerned, but after seeing the loopy smiles Jennifer and I both wore, her expression changed to one I recognized from when I was a little boy. I could read her eyes as if they were computer screens. *What's going on, Anthony? Don't do this to me.*

One of her bosses stepped in front of her with a new supply of chips for the game. She looked at me over his shoulder; now her eyes were wider and even more expressive, more emphatic. *Anthony, what's going on?*

She counted down the money in the lockbox, concentrating since she knew the guard and security cameras overhead were watching her. As she got set to deal a new game, I leaned forward and put something on the table. She thought I had placed a bet, except I hadn't put down cash. My mom saw it was a check, and then on closer inspection saw it was made out to her.

"What's this?" she asked.

"Clock out, Mom," I said.

Now she was even more confused. So was the security guard, who peeked at the check over my mom's shoulder.

"What are you talking about?" she asked.

"Look at the check," I said. "You're through."

"What do you mean?"

"Clock out," I said. "You're done working."

"I can't leave," she said. "I have four people at the table, security, the cameras, the money . . ."

She started to cry.

"You can leave," I said. "You're done."

It took my mom a few minutes to understand that her train had just pulled into the station. Her career had just ended. She no longer had to work. In the event she didn't get it, though, I explained it to her. As of a moment ago, she was officially retired. Free to do whatever she wanted. Sit at home. Play with her grandchildren. Travel the world. Her life belonged to her. I had never felt as good or been as happy. The four people at my mom's table seemed to be enjoying the moment, too. One woman clapped and offered her congratulations. The guy next to her gave me a shrug and asked, "How about me, too?"

Jennifer and I watched as my mom found her boss and turned in her resignation, effective immediately. She was trying not to smile and laugh and failing miserably at both. Confused, her boss followed her back to the table. She introduced me and we shook hands.

"My son is retiring me," she told him.

"You can't just walk out," he said.

"Well, I guess I can now," she said.

A woman clapped. Others joined in.

"Go for it!" someone said.

Crying, my mom walked out of the pit and hugged Jennifer and me. Now the people who had been playing at her table were applauding with more enthusiasm. She waved goodbye to them, and the casino, as I hoisted her into my arms and carried her out like Richard Gere and Debra Winger at the end of *An Officer and a Gentleman*.

"Anthony, you're crazy," she said.

"No, I'm really lucky."

Outside, she continued to wipe tears off her face.

"What am I going to do now?" she asked.

"Whatever you want," I said. "The world is yours."

54

It's now a hot summer day in 2011, and I have taken my sons to a sporting goods store. I have three sons: Dawson, eleven; Evan, eight; and Noah, four. They're my team. They run into the store literally bursting with enthusiasm. I catch their excitement. This is the kind of outing I would've killed to have gone on with my dad. What's better than looking at shelves of baseballs, footballs, basketballs, bicycles, fishing rods, and pool toys? It's all fuel for fun, dreams, and the possibility of heroics that can be replayed forever. After seeing a shelfful of soccer balls, I pictured myself kicking goals back in the day.

"Dad, this is so cool!" Dawson says loudly. "Come look at this."

I have no idea where any of the boys have gone.

"Dawson, where are you guys?" I ask.

"Over here," he says.

"Thanks, that helps a lot," I say, laughing. "Where's 'over here'?"

Though I've temporarily lost my boys in a sporting goods store, I have a firm grasp on where I am in my life. Six years have passed since Daniel Holstein called to ask if I knew an Eddie Zuiker, and although I didn't know it at the time, it turned into an opportunity for me to get to know my dad and figure out who I am—and to figure out whether or not I had turned into the man I wanted to be when I grew up. Now I'm all about being a dad. My boys are always at the top of my to-do list. Once you're a parent, you're no longer the day's number one priority— and if you are, as I frequently remind myself, you're not doing it right.

Despite the enormous success of the *CSI* franchise (in 2011, it was named the most-watched TV series in the world—the third time in four years it had earned that distinction), I still work like I'm the new kid in town. I don't know any other way. I returned to the original show and wrote new episodes with Carol, as we had more than a decade earlier, and I had a blast. I launched my own production company, Dare to Pass, with Matt Weinberg, a colleague from back in the Globetrotter days, as president, and my longtime assistant and friend Orlin as vice president.

I have also branched out into publishing, the Internet, the world of apps and mobile devices, and speaking engagements, where I share the ride of my life, from the tram driver to *CSI*. As those who've heard me speak already know, the best lessons are the simplest. Don't give up. Your gift is your passion. Less money can turn into more. Catchy slogans, of course, don't change lives. That's up to you. This book, for instance, which was supposed to be about achieving success, turned into a father-son story that resolved itself better than the tragedy it would seem to be.

Most people have a tale of estrangement, anger, or bitterness about someone or something similar to the way I felt about Eddie. My advice? Drop it. Learn to let it go and concentrate on what you can do, not what you can't. Build your life till you're the success you've dreamed about.

My friends have done it. Rico built a real estate business, Manzo became a successful entreprenuer, and Dustin turned to writing and became an Emmy-nominated writer on *CSI*. All of us learned similar lessons. Don't get down on yourself when life presents challenges. Although there will always be obstacles, frustrations, and wrong turns, understand they're a necessary part of the learning process, of figuring out where you're supposed to end up.

My success is now defined by one word: *fatherhood*.

Unlike me, my boys will always know they're loved and supported by their dad. As they face their own challenges, they'll have me on the sidelines, where I wished my father would've been.

One day they'll learn the truth about Eddie and the credit he deserves for helping to make me the man I am today. His failures as a father motivated me to grab on to anything remotely positive, and filled me with a rage that I managed to channel into a will to succeed. Without my mom, I probably would've gone off the rails. But she taught me to do the right thing—and that, in retrospect, is the takeaway between Eddie and me.

As a result, here I am in a sporting goods store with my

boys. As they play with footballs, I marvel at the second, third, and fourth chances life affords you to be your best if you stay on the right path. To me, that's the real tragedy of Eddie's failure. He didn't realize that it's never too late. At least I know Dawson and his brothers will tell a story about a close relationship with their father.

POSTSCRIPT

Originally, I wanted to write a self-help book that answered the question most frequently asked of me—how'd you do it? How did you go from driving a tram at the Mirage hotel for eight bucks an hour when you were twenty-six years old to creating the most profitable franchise in TV history, *CSI: Crime Scene Investigation*? I understand what's really underlying the question: People look at me and see an ordinary guy with everyday tastes who had an idea and made it happen, and they want to know how I did it so they can do it, too.

The problem with a self-help book is that each of us has to write our own. Otherwise it wouldn't be *self-help*. So as you no doubt discovered, I didn't write that type of book. I wrote my story. That's what I advise you to do, too. Live your life as if you're writing a story. Keep in mind there's no right or wrong way.

As I discovered and you will, too, no one can tell you which turns are right or wrong. You'll figure that out on your own. You'll know it. Do what you love, keep the faith, and remember you are your single best resource. You can't make others believe in you unless you believe in yourself.

ACKNOWLEDGMENTS

As you can see, the road to success is not a lonely one, and I have been incredibly blessed to have had, and still have, incredible people supporting me along the way. There is no way I would be where I am today if it weren't for their help and encouragement. While many people are highlighted in such a way throughout the book, there are a number of people I would specifically like to thank.

First and foremost, my three boys: Dawson, Evan, and Noah, for being the most important people in my life.

My mother, Diana, for doing the best she could and the incredible sacrifices she made for me growing up. My grandmother, for always being the first to hear my pitches and being brutally honest with her notes.

Kudos to Team Zuiker; my manager Margaret Riley; my agents Joe Cohen, Steve Lafferty, Jon Ringquist, Scott Greenberg, Ophir Lupu, Seamus Blackley, Peter Jacobs, and Shari Smiley; my book agent, Dan Strone; my lawyers, Kevin Yorn, Alex Kohner, and Nick Gladden; my business manager, Harley Neuman. Thanks for always watching out for me, always steering me in the best direction (even if it's not always the direction I wanted to go), and helping me build a career that a kid in Vegas could have only dreamed of.

A very special thanks to my mentor, the late Bernie Brillstein.

I'd like to thank Leslie Moonves for giving me my first big break, Nina Tassler for giving me my first "yes," and, of course, Nancy Tellem. And thank you to William Peterson for giving a no-name kid from Vegas the nod. I will never forget how you kept your word.

I'd also like to thank Carol Mendelsohn, Ann Donahue, and Pam Veasey for being the greatest show runners on the planet. Thanks to Danny Cannon for shooting an amazing pilot. Many thanks to Cynthia Chvatal. Daniel Holstein, you opened up a world to me I never knew existed.

To Jerry Bruckheimer and Jonathan Littman for signing on with an untested TV writer and helping turn the *CSI* franchise into a cultural and ratings phenomenon.

Team Dare to Pass: Matthew Weinberg, Orlin Dobreff, David Boorstein, and Joshua Caldwell. Though this book is about my past, Dare to Pass is my future. Thanks for all your help and support, for challenging me and pushing me as we set out on our own journey in Hollywood.

Thanks to everyone at CBS Network: Christina Davis, Bobby Zotnowski, Bryan Seabury.

Thanks to everyone at CBS/Paramount: David Stapf, Julie McNamara, Leigh Redman.

The cast and crew of the *CSI* franchise: (*CSI*) Laurence Fishburne, Marg Helgenberger, George Eads, Paul Guilfoyle, Eric Szmanda, Robert David Hall, Jorja Fox, Gary Dourdan, Wallace Langham, Archie Kao, David

Berman, Liz Vassey; (*CSI: Miami*) David Caruso, Emily Procter, Adam Rodriguez, Rex Linn, Jonathan Togo, Khandi Alexander, Eva La Rue; (*CSI:NY*) Gary Sinise, Carmine Giovinazzo, Hill Harper, Eddie Cahill, Melina Kanakaredes, Anna Belknap, Robert Joy, A. J. Buckley, and Sela Ward. While the *CSI* series started out as words on the page, you brought it to life and gave the audience a reason to care.

Additional thanks to Joy Fehily, Maria Herrera, and Tracy Shafer.

To Don Epstein and Michael Steele, thanks for giving me the opportunities to share my story time and time again.

Thank you to Anthony Manzo, Americo Longo III, and Dustin Lee Abraham for giving me my start. You guys believed in me first.

Thanks to my partner in this book, Todd Gold; you're as solid as your name. Great job! And to the following people at HarperCollins: Jonathan Burnham, David Hirshey, and Barry Harbaugh. Many thanks for believing in this book from the beginning.

And finally, a very special thanks to my stepfather, David Orfin. While Eddie was never there for me, David was, and he has been an incredible husband to my mother and a father to me. While Eddie made me want to be a better father than he was, it was David who showed me how.

ABOUT THE AUTHOR

Anthony E. Zuiker is the creator and executive producer of the most watched television show in the world, *CSI: Crime Scene Investigation*, as well as *CSI: Miami* and *CSI: NY*. He is also the author of the bestselling novels *Level 26: Dark Origins*, *Dark Prophecy*, and *Dark Revelations*. Zuiker is a visionary business leader who speaks professionally about the future of entertainment and storytelling on multiple platforms. He lives in Los Angeles, California.